FAVOURITE
FUNNY
STORIES

Research by Hilary McGough

KINGFISHER
An imprint of Kingfisher Publications Plc
New Penderel House, 283–288 High Holborn
London WC1V 7HZ
www.kingfisherpub.com

First published by Kingfisher 2003
2 4 6 8 10 9 7 5 3 1

A CIP catalogue record for this book
is available from the British Library.

ISBN 0 7534 0899 6

Printed in India
ITR/0703/THOM/BS(MAR)/90WF

FAVOURITE FUNNY STORIES

CHOSEN BY
ROGER McGOUGH

ILLUSTRATED BY
ADAM STOWER

KINGFISHER

CONTENTS

A FOREWORD OF WARNING

I HOPE YOU WILL ENJOY READING these funny stories; if not, you are in deep, deep trouble. I mean, it took my wife, Hilary, and I ages to read stories from all over the world in order to find the best ones. Then I had to type them all out so that my editor, Miranda Baker, could check through before sending them to Adam Stower so that he could do his wonderful drawings. Next, the manuscript had to be typeset and printed, and no sooner had I done that than it was publishing day and I had to drive round all the bookshops and put the books up on the shelves. It's not easy, you know. And do I get any thanks off you lot? I should be so lucky.

But anyway, I hope you'll agree all that work I put in was worth it. Some of these stories are complete in themselves, from the wild slapstick of Andy Griffiths to the joyful silliness of Terry Jones, from the wondrous weirdness of Margaret Mahy to the giggly spookiness of Roald Dahl. Others are extracts taken from full-length novels from some of the funniest writers around – Judy Blume, Morris Gleitzman, Mark Twain, Allan Ahlberg (to mention only two) – which I hope will encourage you to rush to your local bookshop or library, in order to read the whole story.

And another thing. I thought I'd better warn you that plain-clothes police from the Laughter Squad are on the prowl, and anybody found in possession of this book and wearing a gloomy face may be arrested and charged under the Comedy Act. You have been warned!

ROGER McGOUGH
May 2003

IN THE SHOWER WITH ANDY

ANDY GRIFFITHS

I 'M IN THE SHOWER. Singing. And not just because the echo makes my voice sound so cool either. I'm singing because I'm so happy.

Ever since I've been old enough to have showers I've been trying to find a way to fill a shower cubicle up with water. If I put a face-washer over the plughole I can get the water as far up as my ankles, but it always ends up leaking out through gaps in the door.

But I think I've finally found the answer – Dad's silicone gun.

I've plugged up the plughole.

I've sealed up the shower-screen doors.

I've even filled in all the cracks in the tiles.

The cubicle is completely watertight and the water is already up to my knees.

And the best thing is that I've got all night to enjoy it.

Mum and Dad have got Mr and Mrs Bainbridge over for dinner. They'll be too busy listening to Mr Bainbridge talking about himself to have time to worry about what I'm doing.

I hear banging on the door.

"Have you almost finished, Andy?"

It's Jen!

9

"No", I say. "I think I'm going to be in here a while yet."

"Can you hurry up?" yells Jen.

"But you already had your shower this morning," I yell.

"I'm going out," she says. "I need the bathroom!"

"OK. I'll be out in a minute," I call. I always say that. It's the truth. Sort of. I will be out in a minute – I'm just not saying which minute it will be.

The cubicle is filling with thick white steam. Just the way I like it. Dad's always telling us how important it is to turn the fan on when we're having a shower, but I can't see the point. A shower without steam doesn't make sense. You might as well go and stand outside in the rain.

My rubber duck bumps against my legs. I pick it up.

"This is it," I say. "Just you and me . . . going where no boy – or rubber duck – has ever gone before."

It has its bill raised in a sort of smile. It must be as excited as I am. Let's face it, there can't be that much excitement in the life of a rubber duck. Except that you'd get to see everybody without their clothes on.

Jen bangs on the door again.

"Andy! Pleeeeease!"

"OK," I call. "I'll be out in a minute."

"You said that a minute ago!"

"I'm washing my hair."

"But you've been in there for at least half an hour. You don't have *that* much hair."

"I'm using a new sort of shampoo – I have to do it strand by strand."

"Andy!"

The water is almost up to my belly-button. There's only one thing missing. Bubbles!

I pick up the bubble bath and measure out a capful. I tip it into the water. A few bubbles, but not enough. I add another cap. And another. And another. One more for good measure. Another for good luck.

I keep adding bubble bath until the bottle is empty. The bubbles rise over my head. Cool. It's like I am being eaten by this enormous white fungus. Well, not that being eaten by an enormous white fungus would be cool – it would probably be quite uncool, actually – but you know what I mean.

Jen is yelling.

"Andy, if you don't get out right this minute, you're going to be sorry."

Jen is persistent, I'll give her that. But I'll fix her. I'll use my old "what did you say?" routine.

"Pardon?" I yell. "What did you say?"

"I said you're going to be sorry!"

"What? I can't hear you!"

"I said get out of the shower!"

"Pardon?"

No reply. I win.

Aaaagghhh!

The water's gone hot! Boiling hot!

Jen must have flushed the toilet. That's bad news.

I lose.

I jump back against the shower wall.

Hot water splatters onto my face. My chest. My arms.

I grab the cold tap and turn it on full.

The hot water disappears. Now it's freezing.

I'm going to have turn both taps off and start all over again. I hate that. Being a pioneer is not easy.

I turn the hot tap off. But the cold won't budge.

I grab the tap with both hands. I try to twist it clockwise but it's stuck. Not even my super-strength can move it.

The silicone gun is hanging off the shower pipe. I pick it up and start bashing the tap with it. That should loosen it.

But the handgrip shatters.

The pieces disappear into the soapy water. I'm staring at a thin metal rod coming out of the wall. And the water is still flowing full blast.

I kneel down and clamp my teeth over the tap rod.

No good. The tap feels like it's rusted into place. My teeth will crack before it moves.

There's no steam left. The bubbles have been flattened.

11

The freezing water is almost up to my chest. Maybe this wasn't such a great idea.

Time to bail out.

I take a deep breath and dive to the bottom of the shower. I'm trying to find the plughole. I've got to get the silicone out before the shower fills up completely.

But I can't do it. I did the job too well. There's nothing but a hard rubbery slab of silicone where the plug used to be. I can't poke through it. I can't get a fingernail underneath to lift up. It's times like this I wish I didn't bite my nails. But then it's times like this that cause me to bite my nails in the first place.

I stand up, gasping for air. The water is up to my neck. I grab hold of the doorhandle and try to wrench it open but I laid the silicone even thicker on the doors than the plughole. If you ever want anything sealed tight I can recommend Dad's silicone gun. This stuff stays stuck forever.

I'm going to have to break the door down.

I'll use the gun. It made short work of the tap so the door shouldn't be a problem.

I bash the glass with the gun handle. It bounces off. I bash it again, harder this time. The gun snaps in two. Just my luck. Reinforced shower screen glass. Unbreakable.

I'm shivering. And not just from the cold. I'm scared.

I start bashing the door with the duck.

"HELP! I'M DROWNING! HELP!"

"I'm not surprised!" Jen yells back. "You've been in there long enough."

"Jen, I'm not kidding. Help me!"

"What did you say?" she says. "I can't hear you."

"Be serious," I yell. "I've siliconed myself in here."

"What?"

She wins again.

I'm treading water. My head is very close to the top of the shower.

The only way I can save myself is to get rid of the water.

I'm going to have to drink it.

Dirty soapy shower water.

I'd rather die.

The water nudges the tip of my nose.

Actually, on second thoughts I'd rather drink the water.

I start swallowing.

It's working. I just have to drink as fast as the shower is filling up. And if I can drink even faster then I might get out of here alive yet. Actually the water doesn't taste that bad – it's only been three days since my last shower.

I keep swallowing.

And swallowing. And swallowing. And swallowing.

Uh-oh.

I can't believe this.

I need to go to the toilet.

But I can't.

I'll drink dirty shower water but I won't drink that.

I've got to hold on.

But I can't do that, either.

I'm busting.

My head is bumping against the roof of the shower.

It's getting harder to breathe.

There's more banging on the door but it sounds like it's coming from a long way away.

"I'm going to tell Dad," says Jen in a distant voice. "Is that what you want? Is it?"

"Yes, Jen," I call. "Yes! Please hurry!"

Everything becomes quiet.

My life is flashing before my eyes.

I see myself blowing a high-pitched whistle while Mum is trying to talk on the telephone. I see myself letting down the tyres on Dad's car. I see myself hiding a rubber snake in Jen's bed. Is that all I did with my life? Annoy people? Surely I did something useful . . . something good?

Nope. I can't think of anything. Except for solving the problem of how to fill a shower cubicle with water.

I may be going to die, but at least it will be a hero's death. Future generations of Australian children will thank me as they float around in their sealed-up shower cubicles.

Ouch!

Something is pressing into the top of my head.

I look up.

The fan! I forgot all about it.

It's not very big, but it's better than nothing. If I can get the grille off then I can escape through the hole and up into the roof.

I work my fingers under the edge of the grille and pull on it. It comes off easily.

I reach into the casing and grab hold of the fan. I rock it back and forth. There is a little bit of give in it. I start giving it all I've got.

Finally the bolts holding it give way. I push my arms and head into the hole, kicking like mad to get the thrust I need to make it all the way up.

The opening is smaller than I thought. I expel every last bit of air in my lungs to make myself thin enough to fit through the hole. Not that there was much air left in them, but it seems to help.

At last! I'm through!

I'm lying on a yellow insulation batt in the roof of our house. The glass fibres are prickly on my skin, but I'm not complaining. It's a lot better than where I was. I look back into the hole. It's like one of those fishing holes that Eskimos cut in the ice. But there's no fish. Just my rubber duck. I reach down and pick it out. We're in this together. I can't just leave it.

After I get my breath back I look around.

I know there's a manhole in the top of the kitchen. All I have to do is locate it, climb down into the kitchen and nick down the hallway into my room. Then I can put my pyjamas on and go to bed early. It will save a lot of boring explanation – and, if I'm really lucky, Jen will get the blame.

I have to move fast. I start crawling towards the kitchen. I'm carrying the duck in one hand and using my other hand to feel my way along the roof beam.

Suddenly I feel a sharp pain in my thumb. I jerk my hand back and almost lose my balance. I fling the duck away so I can grab the beam with my other hand.

I look at my thumb. A huge splinter is sticking out of it. I pull it out with my teeth. Ouch!

I shake my hand a few times and look around for my duck. It has landed in the middle of a large unsupported section of insulation batts. I'm tempted to leave it there. But that wouldn't be right. It's been with me all the way. I can't abandon it now.

I reach towards it but it's too far away. I'm going to have to crawl out there. I know you're not supposed to climb on the unsupported parts of the roof, but I think it will be OK. I'm not that heavy. And it's not as if I have any clothes on to weigh me down.

I climb carefully onto the batts and start moving slowly to the centre. One more metre and I'm there.

I pick up my duck and bring it up to my face. "Just you and me," I say.

The duck creaks. That's weird. I didn't know rubber ducks could talk.

Uh-oh. The creaking is not coming from the duck. It's coming from underneath me. The ceiling is giving away.

I try to grab the roof beam but I can't reach it.

The ceiling caves in.

Next thing I know I'm lying, legs spread, in the middle of the dinner table – my fall broken by an insulation batt.

As the dust from the ceiling plaster settles, I see Mr and Mrs Bainbridge and Mum and Dad staring down at me.

Jen is standing next to Dad, her bath towel draped over her shoulder. Her back is turned towards me and she's so busy complaining to Dad that she doesn't seem to notice what has happened.

". . . I've asked him a million times but he just won't get out . . ." she's saying.

"Oh, dear," says Mum.

"Oh, my," says Mrs Bainbridge.

For once in his life Mr Bainbridge is speechless.

"Oh, no," says Dad, shaking his head at me. "No, no, no!"

"Oh yes," says Jen. "And I'll tell you what else . . ."

Dad nods in my direction.

Jen stops, turns around and stares.

I cover myself with the rubber duck, swing my legs over the edge of the table and stand up.

"I beg your pardon," I say. "I was looking for the kitchen."

Nobody says anything. They are all just staring at me, their faces and clothes white from the plaster dust.

I head towards the door as fast as I can.

As I'm about to exit I turn towards Jen. She is still standing there, eyes wide.

"Well, what are you waiting for?" I say. "Shower's free!"

WOOF!

ALLAN AHLBERG

Imagine what it would be like to turn into a dog. Just like that. One minute you're a boy, the next you're a Norfolk terrier! This extract describes the first of Eric's many hilarious canine adventures.

THERE WAS ONCE A BOY who turned into a dog. This doesn't happen every day. If it did, the world would soon be short of boys and overrun with dogs. What's more, it would hardly be a story worth telling. It would be like: There was once a boy who had his breakfast; or: There was once a boy who walked down the road. Luckily – for story-tellers, at least – that isn't the way of it. There are common happenings in this world, and uncommon. So . . .

There was once a boy who turned into a dog. The boy's name was Eric Banks; he was ten years old. The dog he turned into was a Norfolk terrier.

Eric Banks was a quiet boy, most of the time: "steady worker", "methodical", his school reports said. He was the kind of boy who didn't make a rush for the back seat of the bus, or go mad when the first snow fell. He was left-handed, right-footed and rather small for his age. He had freckles.

Eric lived with his parents and his little sister; her name was

Emily; she was three. His dad was a postman; his mum had a part-time job in a shop. Eric himself had a paper-round which he shared with his friend, Roy Ackerman. (Actually, he was too young to have the round. It belonged to his cousin. But she had broken her arm, and Eric's dad was a friend of the newsagent . . . so, Eric was standing in.)

Eric first turned into a dog a little at a time in his own bed. His parents were downstairs watching television. His sister was fast asleep in the next room. The time was ten past nine; the day, Wednesday; the month June. Until then it had been a normal day for Eric. He'd done his paper-round with Roy, and gone to school. He'd had two helpings of his favourite dinner. He'd played with Emily before tea, and Roy after. He'd watched television, had a shower and gone to bed. Now he was *in* bed and turning into a dog.

It happened like this. Eric was lying on his side with his eyes closed. He was almost asleep. Suddenly, he felt an itch inside the collar of his pyjama jacket. This – although he didn't know it yet – was the fur sprouting. He felt a curious tingling in his hands and feet. This was his hands and feet turning into paws. He felt his nose becoming cold and wet, his ears becoming flappy. Eric opened his eyes. He didn't panic straight away. This was his nature, partly, but also he was still half-asleep. The thought in his mind was: "I'm turning into a dog!"

That was another thing about Eric: he was a good guesser. When Emily first learned to talk, it was usually Eric who guessed what she was trying to say. He could guess the mood his teacher was in, just from the way she held her hymn-book in assembly. Now – on the evidence of a furry paw where his hand should have been – he guessed he was turning into a dog. He didn't suppose he was turning into a *werewolf*, for instance, which is what Roy Ackerman would have thought. He didn't suppose he was dreaming, either, which he was not.

The time it took Eric to turn into a dog – his shape blurring and rippling like a swimmer under water – was about fifteen seconds. The time it took him to become frantic was about five seconds after that. His first action was to begin scrabbling in the bed, trying to get a better look at himself. His thoughts were in a turmoil: "I'm a dog! A *dog*." The next thing he did was try to get out of bed. This wasn't easy for a dog in pyjamas; besides, they were baggy on him now. Eric leapt, and landed in a heap. He kicked his way clear of the trousers and backed out of the jacket. He resisted the urge to growl when one of his claws got caught in a buttonhole. He sat on the floor and thought: "I'm a dog!"

It was now a quarter past nine. The last of the evening sunlight was shining through the green curtains. Everything in the room – furniture and wallpaper, Eric's books and toys, his junior science kit, his clothes laid out on a chair beside the bed – was tinged with green light. Birds were chirruping outside the window. Next door, Mr Phipps was mowing his lawn.

Eric got to his feet – all four of them – and walked uncertainly across the room. He put his front paws on the dressing-table and stared into the mirror. A furry, rather surprised-looking face stared back. "I don't believe it," he thought, and then: "I look like a Norfolk terrier." Eric knew a bit about dogs. He'd done a project on them with Roy in the second year.

Once more Eric sat on the floor. He was bewildered, to say the least. A confusion of questions jostled in his head: "How could it happen? What's the cause of it? Why me?" He went to the window, put his paws on the sill, ducked his head under the curtain and looked out. Mr Phipps was emptying the grass cuttings onto a compost heap. A whisp of blue smoke was rising from a bonfire in the next garden along. Eric left the window, and – with no clear aim in mind – nudged open the bedroom door with his head. He went onto the landing. He couldn't see much – it was gloomy – but he could smell all kinds of things. There were biscuit crumbs in the carpet. There was talcum powder. He felt the urge to sniff around. Soon he came upon a chocolate button which his sister must have dropped. She had been eating them earlier that evening. Eric studied the button. At that moment the thought in his mind was: "Being a dog might not be *all* bad." And he ate it up.

Eric sat at the top of the stairs. He had sniffed around for other chocolate buttons without success. He'd been tempted to try his luck in Emily's room – her door was ajar as usual – but decided not to risk it. Besides, the prospects weren't good. Emily dropping her sweets was common; Emily leaving them was rare.

Now Eric cocked his head to one side. From the room below he could hear the television. In the kitchen his dad was making supper. There was a smell of coffee and cold meat. Eric felt his mouth watering, and – all at once – came to a decision: he would tell his mum and dad, that was the thing to do! After all, it wasn't as if he'd done anything wrong; wrong had been done to him.

Eric began to go downstairs. The thought occurred to him: "I wonder what's on?" And then: "Perhaps I can stay up, since I'm a dog." But going down stairs isn't easy for a dog, especially an inexperienced one. Eric found his stomach was dragging on the steps and being tickled by the carpet. What was worse, his back legs kept catching up with his front. On the last few steps he took a tumble, skidded on the hall mat and bumped into the coat-stand. After that, the sitting-room door opened, the hall light went on – it was gloomy there, too – and Eric's mum appeared.

Mrs Banks looked down at him. "Charles!" she called. "We've got a dog in the house!"

A moment later Mr Banks appeared in the kitchen doorway. He saw a worried-looking Norfolk terrier on the hall mat. (Mr Banks knew about dogs. He was a postman, remember.) He crouched down and held out a hand. "Now then," he said; "how did *you* get in?"

Eric peered up at his parents. He was surprised so see how enormous they were. Their feet were huge; their heads up near the ceiling. And he was surprised that they didn't know him. Of course, there was a good reason for this, but even so . . .

Eric advanced towards his father's outstretched hand and began to speak. "I didn't get in, Dad – it's me, Eric – I've turned into a dog!"

Well, that's certainly what Eric meant to say. It's what was in his mind. However, what came out was just a string of barks and yelps. Eric tried again. It was no use. The trouble was, he had the brains of a boy, the thoughts of a boy, but the vocal chords of a dog. Mr Banks patted his head. It occurred to him that he had seen this dog before. Its expression was . . . familiar.

Now Eric, in desperation, began prancing about. He had the idea of somehow *miming* who he was, or at least showing his parents that here was no ordinary dog. The effect was convincingly dog-like. Mrs Banks patted him also. "It's almost like he was trying to tell us something," she said. (She was a good guesser, too; unfortunately, on this occasion, not good enough.)

"Yes," said Mr Banks. "Perhaps he's trying to tell us how he got in." He took hold of Eric by the scruff of the neck and began leading him towards the door. "Come on, out you go!"

Eric didn't like the sound of this. He barked and whined. He dragged his feet.

"Sh!" said Mrs Banks. "Bad dog – you'll wake the children!"

"I *am* the children," barked Eric, "or one of them – or I was!" He struggled on a little longer. Then, sensing the hopelessness of the situation (he could hardly bite his own father), Eric gave up. He allowed himself to be led from the house and down the front path. Mrs Banks went on ahead and opened the gate. Mr Banks pushed him out onto the pavement. "Off you go," he said, and clapped his hands. "Shoo!"

Reluctantly, Eric shuffled off a few steps, then sat down. When his parents' backs were turned, he pushed his head through a gap in the fence. He watched them as they returned to the house. He heard his mum say, "I wonder how he *did* get in?" He saw the front door close.

Eric rested his muzzle on the bottom rail of the fence, and felt hard done by. A warm breeze ruffled the fur along his back. Garden smells assailed his nose. He pricked his ears to catch the distant chiming of an ice-cream van. Someone across the road was playing a piano; someone was laughing. Eric stared forlornly at his own front door. He began to think of ways to get back in.

Just then a young cat came sauntering round the corner out of Clay Street. The cat saw Eric and Eric saw the cat more or less at the same time. The cat, though inexperienced, knew what was called for: it turned and ran. Eric didn't hesitate either. Here he was, a dog; abandoned on the street by his own parents *because* he was a dog. What else was he to do? It wasn't his fault. He ran after the cat.

Eric didn't catch the cat, though he tried hard enough. He chased it down Clay Street and into Apollo Road. He almost cornered it by the Ebenezer Chapel. He only lost it at the scout hut. At the scout hut, the cat left the pavement and ran up an eight-foot fence instead. (An older cat would have done something of the kind sooner.) Eric skidded to a halt. He barked and pranced about at the foot of the fence. The cat glared at him from the top, swished its tail and disappeared.

Eric stopped prancing. He barked half-heartedly at the spot where the cat had been. Now that he had time to think, he was embarrassed. He looked up and down the street to see if anyone was watching. He had his tongue out, panting – more embarrassment! Across the street, a man and a dog came out of one of the houses. Eric recognized the dog. It was a bull-mastiff he sometimes had trouble with on his paper-round. His dad had trouble with it, too. The mastiff spotted him and began barking fiercely and straining on its lead. Eric couldn't understand the barks in detail, but the general meaning was clear. When he could see which way the man and dog were going, he hurried off in the opposite direction. From a safe distance he allowed himself a defiant bark for the mastiff's benefit.

Eric trotted on. He glanced back once or twice to check that he was not pursued. He began to think about his troubles. "That cat distracted me. I've got no reason to be running the streets." He was in Vernon Street now, and heading up towards the park. "Yet if I go home, I'll be put out again."

Eric slowed down and finally stopped. He looked around in a baffled way. There was an interesting smell of sausage roll in the air. He ignored it. Overhead the sky was cloudless and full of light, though it was getting late, half-past nine at least. Suddenly, Eric thought of something. He remembered the writing he'd seen scrawled on the fence which the cat had run up:

DOWN WITH THE VILLA, P.L. LOVES R.V., and so on. He remembered reading it. Well – and this was the point – if he could read, he could *write*. He could go home and scratch a message in the dirt: "S.O.S. ERIC" or just "ERIC", that would do. "Mum and Dad aren't stupid," he thought. "They'd never get rid of a dog who could write their own son's name in the – he had another idea – "Emily's sandpit, that was the place!"

Eric at once became impatient to try out his idea. Luckily, on Vernon Street there were grass verges between the front gardens and the pavement. He soon found a bare patch suitable for this purpose. He looked around. Two girls with tennis rackets were coming down the street. He waited for them to pass. A woman with a pram went by on the opposite side. A car and a couple of cyclists came and went. Then it was clear.

Eric sat up straight and extended his left paw. He brushed a sweet-paper and a bit of twig from his chosen spot. He began to write. "E . . . R . . .," he scratched his letters in the dusty earth. It reminded him of the sand-tray at Mrs Parry's playschool years ago. "It's going to work," he thought. "E . . . R . . . I . . . C . . . I can do it!"

When he'd finished, Eric put his head on one side and stared at the result. "Needs to be neater, though – that R's no good." He scrubbed out what he had written and began again. He became for a time engrossed in the quality of his writing. (If Mrs Jessop – she was his teacher – could've seen him then! Eric was not always so particular.)

All of a sudden he was aware of being watched. He heard a voice say, "Here, Jack – come and look at this dog." From the nearby garden a large woman was peering at him over a hedge. She had her hair in rollers and was holding a watering can. "He's writing – in the dirt!"

From the direction of the house a man's voice said, "Geroff!"

"Yes he is – he's stopped now – he's scrubbing it out!"

"Geroff!" said the man.

Eric considered the situation, and decided to leave. He set off up the street. "E . . . R . . . I . . . C," he heard the woman say. 'Eric', that's what he wrote."

"Geroff!" the man said. There was a burst of laughter. "That's no name for a dog!"

Eric sat on his haunches and peered through a gap in the fence. As he did so, he noticed two things: one, his mum was in the garden, watering the roses; two, the front door was open! That was enough for Eric. In no time at all he had changed his plan. He would sneak into the house instead, if he could, and hide in his room. He could write the message in the morning. His chances would be better then. He could reach the back of the house. It would be light. Besides, there was the prospect of curling up on his own bed, and no bull-mastiff to bother him. With this in mind, Eric was encouraged to try his luck.

The first stage proved easy. He wriggled under the bottom rail of the fence and crept along behind the cover of the rose bushes. His mum was humming a tune and had her back to him. He reached the safety of the hall.

Then there was his dad to watch out for. But that proved easy, too. He was in the bathroom, shaving. Postmen have to get up early, and Eric's dad often shaved at night to save time in the morning. Eric crept upstairs to the landing. His bedroom door had swung to, so that it looked more or less shut. He nudged it open and went inside. The light from a street lamp shone faintly through the curtains. His pyjamas – that Eric supposed he would never wear again – still lay in a heap on the floor. He was surprised once more by how big everything looked: the huge chair with his huge clothes on it; the giant bed looming above him.

Eric gathered himself and leapt onto the bed. He turned round a few times to find a comfortable position. He put his head on his paws. The air was heavy with the smell of blanket and sheet, and Airfix glue. There was a half-finished model of a moon buggy on the dresser. He yawned. "This is better, though if Dad looks in there'll be trouble." He yawned again. "I'm a dog . . . a *dog*!" What'll Mum say when she knows? . . . What'll Roy say? 'Brilliant,' Roy'll say."

Eric heard a faint sound downstairs. It was the front door closing. He felt his eyelids growing heavy. "Will I dream human dreams or dog dreams?" He thought about his auntie's cat, the way its whiskers twitched when *it* was dreaming. He closed his eyes.

At that moment, Eric began to feel a curious tingling in his paws. This – although he didn't know it yet – was his paws turning back into hands and feet. He felt an itch around his neck. This was the fur beginning to get shorter. He felt his nose becoming warm and dry, his ears becoming flat against his head. Eric opened his eyes. He didn't move at first. The thought in his mind was: "I'm turning back into a boy!"

But as soon as the itching and tingling stopped, he shot out of bed and pulled back the curtains. Light from the street lamp poured in. Eric felt a tremendous urge to laugh and shout. No more being thrown out of the house – his troubles were over. He was himself again. He was back!

Then, suddenly, he had another thought: he was standing there with no clothes on. What was worse, he'd been running round the streets with no clothes on. *Girls* had seen him! Eric's face grew hot. Hurriedly, he drew the curtains across, grabbed his pyjamas and put them on. He got back into bed.

Gradually, after that, his embarrassment faded. It wasn't so bad when he thought about it. He'd been covered with fur, after all; and if he'd had a T-shirt and shorts on, he'd have looked sillier. Besides, nobody *knew* it was him. Eric yawned, and yawned again. There was a jumble of thoughts crowding in his head; but he was immensely weary. He turned over on his side. "Wait till morning," he thought. "Wait till Roy hears . . ." He closed his eyes. "Brilliant! . . ." and fell asleep.

WHO NEEDS AN ARIES APE?

WALTER DEAN MYERS

O K, SO I REALLY LOVE OLLIE. I mean, who wouldn't love a six-month-old cocker spaniel with those big, dark eyes and the most absolutely adorable ears in the whole world? The question, at least in my mind, is do I love him more because I'm a Leo and he's a Capricorn? I don't know, but I'll keep him anyway and I think we'll get along just fine. If you're wondering what Ollie's being a Capricorn has to do with anything, I'd have to tell you that it really started with the Taurean cat that Mr Jones, the father of the identicals, sold to Mrs Davis. On second thought, maybe I'd better tell you the whole story just as it happened.

The Jones family moved next door to me in Ellisville three years ago. I remember them moving in just about the time I got my second set of braces. Mr Jones is a tall man, a little on the thin side, and he wears glasses. Nothing special about him particularly. Mrs Jones is really nice. She always waves hello and she knew my name, which is Ginger, even before I told her. Probably heard it from some of the other kids in the neighborhood. One of the really cool things about the Jones family is that they own a pet shop. My father said it wasn't doing too well, but all the kids still liked it. Another neat thing about the

Jones family is that they have two girls my age. And the neat thing about the two girls my age is that they're identical twins.

"You can tell them apart by the way they smile." That's what Billy Moran said. "Denise starts her smile from the left side of her face and Debbie starts her smile from the right side of hers."

That's not true, of course. There was no way that you could tell them apart. The fourteen-year-old identicals, as everyone in the neighborhood calls them, are exactly five feet two inches tall, have brown eyes, and skin that looks as if someone added just a touch of brown to the colour of peaches. They both have dimples too.

I like both of them, and they like me. I guess that's why I was the first one that Denise called when their parents were called away to Waterloo. That's where Mrs Jones was from, and it was her mother who was sick.

"Mom will probably be gone for a couple of days, but Dad'll be back by tomorrow night," Denise said. "We have to feed the animals and make sure all the temperatures are right, stuff like that."

"Are you going to sell pets too?" I asked.

"Dad says we can if a customer comes in and knows what they want," Debbie said. "But he wants us to concentrate on just taking care of the animals while they're gone."

Well, naturally, me being practically the best friend of the identicals, I went over to the store the next morning, which was Saturday. When I got there Debbie had just finished checking the temperature of the water in the fish tanks and made sure that the room temperature was warm enough, and Denise was feeding a positively yucky lizard.

We sat around and talked for a while and listened to some classical music. I wanted to listen to some Michael Jackson tapes, but the identicals said that Michael Jackson's music made the budgies nervous. Then, about four-thirty, in comes Mrs Davis with a little calico kitten.

Now, I've known Mrs Davis for about four years. She used to work in the drugstore over on Elm and Third, but now she's retired.

"I really don't think she likes me very much," Mrs Davis said. "She seems so nervous all the time. I think I should return her before she becomes ill."

"How much did you pay for her?" Debbie (she was wearing a pin with her name on it) asked.

"Oh, that's all right," Mrs Davis said. "Why don't you just write down that I did return the kitten and I'll settle with your father when he returns."

"Yes, ma'am," Denise was rubbing the kitten gently behind the ears before putting her into a cage.

"Well," said Debbie after Mrs Davis had left, "did you see that pin Mrs Davis was wearing? It was shaped like a big crab. Maybe that's why the kitten didn't like her. She was too crabby. Get it?"

"I got it," I said, "but with any luck I'll get rid of it before it turns into something serious!"

"Where does Dad keep his records, Debbie?" Denise asked.

"They're in the back room in that closet near the window," Debbie said. "But you'd better stay away from them. You remember that Dad wasn't even too keen on letting us open the store while he and Mom were gone."

"I'm not going to do anything stupid," Denise said, making a face at her sister. "I just want to see something, that's all."

When Denise went into the back room Debbie started telling me how whenever they got into trouble it was usually her sister's fault. Then we started talking about the new gym teacher, who was very cute but losing his hair. Debbie said that she thought that men lost their hair because they worried too much. I said the only thing they were worried about was that they were losing their hair. That's what I heard my Mom say, anyway.

Then Debbie came out from the back room with a big grin on her face like she knew something special.

"So?" I said. "You look like the cat that just swallowed the –"

"That's a no-no in here," said Debbie, putting her hand over my mouth. "But what did you find out, Denise?"

"You remember that crab that Mrs Davis was wearing?"

"Yes," I said.

"So that means her sign is Cancer," Denise said. "And the kitten is a Taurus. Obviously, they are not compatible."

"You mind telling me what you're talking about?" Debbie asked.

"And how did crabs get into this conversation?" I asked.

"All of you, I'm sure," said Denise, "have heard of the science of astrology."

"The nonscience," Debbie said. "My science teacher says that astrology is just a superstition, that the stars have no effect on how people get along with each other."

"Did I say that the stars had an effect on how people get along with each other?" Denise had her hands on her hips. "Did I? Did I?"

"No, but you were just about to, I bet," Debbie said.

"What I was going to say," Denise said, holding her nose in the air, "is that astrology only works on animals. That's why Mrs Davis didn't get along with the kitten. They were born under the wrong stars. She should have had a Libra kitten, and they would have made it just fine."

"I've never heard of that before," I said.

"There are a lot of things that you have never heard of before, Ginger," Denise said. "But that doesn't make them untrue."

That's what Denise was saying, and I had to admit she was right. But then Denise suggested something that sounded pretty good to me. Or at least it did at the time.

"People return pets a lot. Sometimes they say they've made a mistake and they didn't really want the pet, and sometimes they say that there's something wrong with the animal. Dad says that people expect the animals to be like the trained animals you see in television commercials, or they really don't know what to expect," Denise said, "and that's why they bring them back."

"So?" I said, trying to make it sound intelligent.

"So I bet if we did a survey –" Denise was tapping a pencil against the end of her nose – "we'd find out that they were all the wrong signs."

"How do you find out which are the right signs?" I asked.

That's when Denise brought out this book on astrology with

31

all these signs in it, and which ones should work together, and which ones should play sports together, that kind of thing. Then we tried to figure out which ones would be the ones for pets and their owners, and Debbie figured out that it was probably the same as the ones telling you which person you should marry.

"You don't marry a goldfish," I said. "You put him in a bowl with an air pump and feed him once a day."

"You bring him home and you take care of him for the rest of his life," Denise said. I noticed that the identicals were both getting excited about the idea. "And if it's a watchdog, he takes care of you for the rest of his life too. Sounds like a marriage to me."

Well, it didn't sound much like marriage to me. At least not any marriage that I had heard about. All the same, I found myself agreeing with the identicals that we should make a survey of all the pets that Mr Jones had sold over the last six months. That, I want to tell you, was a lot of pets.

What Mr Jones had was a listing of the exact age of every animal. Sometimes the animal, if it was a pedigreed dog or cat, would have the date of its birth listed on a form. If it wasn't on a form then Mr Jones would either estimate the time of its birth or get it from the breeders.

"That way he can tell the new owner what to expect," Denise said

I guess a lot of people were surprised when either Denise or Debbie called and asked what sign they were. I was surprised that we were doing it, but I was even more surprised when I heard Debbie telling a woman that she would have to bring back a Virgo hamster because it was the wrong sign.

"Did the woman say she was going to bring it back?" I asked.

"This afternoon at three o'clock!" Debbie said, very pleased with herself. She had taken a little white mouse out of its cage and it was clinging to her sweater. "She said she was wondering why it wasn't eating properly."

That's when I looked up me and Ollie. I was born on the twelfth of August, which made me a Leo, and Ollie was born on the third of June, which makes him a Gemini. At first I felt bad, then I decided to fudge it. One of the identicals was on the phone and the other one was looking up the sign of a chimpanzee that Mr Jones had sold to the elementary school. He turned out to be an Aries.

"Now, do we go by the principal's birthdate or the teacher who's taking care of him?" Denise asked.

"Who cares whether or not a monkey is an Aries or not?" I said, still thinking about Ollie.

"He's not a monkey," Denise said, "he's an ape!"

"Well, who needs an Aries ape?"

"That is not the question," the other identical said. "The question is whether or not you're going to help us round up the animals who aren't properly matched."

I wouldn't have helped if I were the only one, because I didn't want to get into any trouble. But the identicals called every kid on the block and some in the class that didn't even live near us and that afternoon we were all going around, rounding up animals.

The plan the identicals had for rounding up the animals seemed fine on paper, but it didn't turn out that way. There were animals everywhere. Jimmy Hunter mixed up three guinea pigs so you couldn't tell the Virgo from the two Aries, and Cathy Brown let the iguana she was picking up slip out of the bag when she walked through Memorial Square, and refused to pick it up because she said she was afraid of getting warts.

Of course, not everyone gave up their pets, but a lot of people did. Mostly you could say that dog people and cat people wouldn't give up their animals. On the other hand, fish people, hamster people, some of the parakeet people, and nearly all of the gerbil people gave them up.

Somebody, probably a Pisces person, called the local newspaper and asked what was going on. Everybody showed up at the Joneses' pet shop at the same time. Two kids came with turtles, a man came with a snake wrapped around his neck, two women came with cats just to have their horoscopes read, a reporter came from the local paper, and Mr and Mrs Jones arrived in their station wagon.

We found out that Mrs Jones' mother was OK over in Waterloo, and that Mr Jones was furious right here in Ellisville. He went around apologizing to all the people who had brought their pets back, and his mouth was smiling, but when he looked at the identicals his eyes weren't smiling, not a bit.

But the funniest thing that happened was that when the story hit the newspaper the next day, people from all over the county started calling Mr Jones and coming to him to buy pets. It seems that a lot of people believe in astrology. Like I said, it wasn't so much the dog people, or the cat people, but a lot of the others. In fact, Mr Jones even started putting little tags around the gerbils' necks, which said things like "Hi, I'm an Aquarian" or "Please love me, I'm a Scorpio". I think it's dumb, but now my father said that the Joneses' pet shop is doing very well, so maybe it isn't.

I'm still best friends with the identicals. The other day I took Ollie down to the shop to have his nails trimmed – you have to do that with a cocker spaniel – and Debbie (or maybe it was Denise) said it was sure lucky that Ollie and I were compatible. I said it sure was, but I couldn't help smiling because according to their charts, we weren't compatible at all. And you know what, I wouldn't swear to this, but I think Ollie smiled too.

THE SNOOKS FAMILY

HARCOURT WILLIAMS

ONE NIGHT Mr and Mrs Snooks were going to bed as usual. It so happened that Mrs Snooks got into bed first, and she said to her husband, "Please, Mr Snooks, would you blow the candle out?" And Mr Snooks replied, "Certainly, Mrs Snooks." Whereupon he picked up the candlestick and began to blow, but unfortunately he could only blow by putting his under lip over his upper lip, which meant that his breath went up to the ceiling instead of blowing out the candle flame.

And he puffed and he puffed and he puffed, but he could not blow it out.

So Mrs Snooks said, "I will do it, my dear," and she got out of bed and took the candlestick from her husband and began to blow. But unfortunately she could only blow by putting her upper lip over her under lip, so that all her breath went down to the floor. And she puffed and she puffed, but she could not blow the candle out.

So Mrs Snooks called their son John. John put on his sky-blue dressing-gown and slipped his feet into his primrose-coloured slippers and came down into his parents' bedroom.

'John, dear," said Mrs Snooks, 'will you please blow out the candle for us? And John said, "Certainly, Mummy."

35

But unfortunately John could only blow out of the right corner of his mouth, so that all his breath hit the wall of the room instead of the candle.

And he puffed and he puffed, but he could not blow out the candle.

So they all called for his sister, little Ann. And little Ann put on her scarlet dressing-gown and slipped on her pink slippers and came down to her parents' bedroom.

"Ann, dear," said Mr Snooks, "will you please blow the candle out for us?" And Ann said, "Certainly, Daddy."

But unfortunately Ann could only blow out of the left side of her mouth, so that all her breath hit the wall instead of the candle.

And she puffed and she puffed, but she could not blow out the candle.

It was just then that they heard in the street below a heavy steady tread coming along the pavement. Mr Snooks threw open the window and they all craned their necks out. They saw a policeman coming slowly towards the house.

"Oh, Mr Policeman," said Mrs Snooks, "will you come up and blow out our candle?" We do so want to go to bed."

"Certainly, Madam," replied the policeman, and he entered and climbed the stairs – blump, blump, blump. He came into the bedroom where Mr Snooks, Mrs Snooks, John Snooks and little Ann Snooks were all standing round the candle which they could *not* blow out.

The policeman then picked up the candlestick in a very dignified manner and, putting his mouth into the usual shape for blowing, puffed out the candle at the first puff. Just like this – PUFF!

The Snooks family all said, "Thank you, Mr Policeman." And the policeman said, "Don't mention it," and turned to go down the stairs again.

"Just a moment, Policeman," said Mr Snooks. "You mustn't go down the stairs in the dark. You might fall." And taking a box of matches, he LIT THE CANDLE AGAIN!

Mr Snooks went down the stairs with the policeman and saw

him out of the door. His footsteps went blump, blump, blump along the quiet street.

John Snooks and little Ann Snooks went back to bed. Mr and Mrs Snooks got into bed again. There was silence for a moment.

"Mr Snooks," said Mrs Snooks, "would you blow out the candle?"

Mr Snooks got out of bed. "Certainly, Mrs Snooks," he said . . . And so on *ad infinitum*.

DOUBLE FUDGE

JUDY BLUME

This extract is taken from the latest in a series of books about the irrepressible Fudge and his long-suffering brother, Peter. Fudge has a new obsession – money – and in true Fudge style the whole family gets dragged in.

WHEN MY BROTHER FUDGE WAS FIVE, he discovered money in a big way. "Hey, Pete," he said one night as I was getting out of the shower. "How much would it cost to buy New York?"

"The city or the state?" I asked, as if it were a serious question.

"Which is bigger?"

"The state, but all the good stuff is in the city." People who don't live in the city might disagree, but I'm a city kind of guy.

"We live in the city, right?" Fudge said. He was sitting on the open toilet seat in his pyjamas.

"You're not *doing* anything, are you?" I asked as I towelled myself dry.

"What do you mean, Pete?"

"I *mean* you're sitting on the toilet, and you haven't pulled down your PJs."

He swung his feet and started laughing. "Don't worry, Pete.

Only Tootsie still poops in her pants." Tootsie is our little sister. She'll be two in February.

Fudge watched as I combed my wet hair. "Are you going someplace?" he asked.

"Yeah, to bed." I got into clean boxers and pulled a T-shirt over my head.

"Then how come you're getting dressed?"

"I'm not getting dressed. Starting tonight, this is what I wear instead of pyjamas. And how come you're still up?"

"I can't go to sleep until you tell me, Pete."

"Tell you what?"

"How much it would cost to buy New York City."

"Well, the Dutch paid about twenty-four dollars for it back in the sixteen hundreds."

"Twenty-four dollars?" His eyes opened wide. "That's all?"

"Yeah, it was a real bargain. But don't get your hopes up. That's not what it would cost today, even if it were for sale, which it's not."

"How do you know, Pete?"

"Believe me, I know!"

"But how?"

"Listen, Fudge, by the time you're twelve there's a lot of stuff you know, and you don't even know how you know it."

He repeated my line. "There's a lot of stuff you know and you don't even know how you know it!" Then he laughed like crazy. "That's a tongue-twister, Pete."

"No, that's just the truth, Fudge."

The next day he was at it again. In the elevator he asked Sheila Tubman, "How much money do you have, Sheila?"

"That's not a polite question, Fudgie," she told him. "Nice people don't talk about their money, especially in these times." Sheila gave me a look like it was my fault my brother has no manners. I hope she's not in my class this year. I hope that *every* year, and every year she's there, like some kind of itch you can't get rid of, no matter how hard you scratch.

"I'm nice," Fudge said, "and I like to talk about money. You want to know how much I have?"

"No," Sheila told him. "It's nobody's business but yours."

He told her anyway. I knew he would. "I have fourteen dollars and seventy-four cents. I mise my money every night before I go to sleep."

"You *mise* your money?" Sheila asked. Then she shook her head at me like it's my fault he thinks mise is a word.

Henry, who runs the elevator in our building, laughed. "Nothing like having a miser in the family."

"You don't have to be a miser, Fudge," Sheila said. "If you like counting money so much, you can work at a bank when you grow up."

"Yeah," Fudge said. "I can work at a bank and mise my money all day long."

Sheila sighed. "He doesn't get it," she said to me.

"He's only five," I reminded her.

"Almost six," he reminded me. Then he tugged Sheila's arm. "Hey, Sheila, you know how much the Dude paid for New York City?"

"The Dude?" Sheila asked. "Is this some kind of joke?"

"Not the *Dude*," I told Fudge. "The *Dutch*."

"His name was Peter Minuit," Sheila said, like the know-it-all she is. "And he paid the Wappinger Indian tribe in trinkets, not cash. Besides, the Indians thought they were going to share the land, not sell it."

"Sharing is good," Fudge said. "Except for money. I'll never share my money. My money is all mine. I love my money!"

"That's a disgusting thing to say," Sheila told him. "You're not going to have any friends if you talk that way."

By then the elevator reached the lobby. "Your brother has no values," Sheila said as we walked to the door of the building. Outside, she turned and headed towards Broadway.

"How much do *values* cost?" Fudge asked me.

"Not everything's for sale," I told him.

"It should be." Then he skipped down to the corner singing, "*Money, money, money, I love money, money, money . . .*"

That's when I knew we were in big trouble.

"It's just a stage," Mom told me later when I pointed out that Fudge is obsessed by money.

"Maybe, but it's still embarrassing," I said. "You better do something before school starts."

But Mom didn't take me seriously until that night at dinner when Dad said, "Please pass the salt, Fudge."

"How much will you give me for it?" Fudge asked. The saltshaker was sitting right in front of him.

"Excuse me," Dad said. "I'm asking for a favour, not hiring someone to do a job."

"If you hire me I'll pass the salt," Fudge said. "How about a dollar?"

"How about nothing?" I said, reaching for the salt and passing it to Dad.

"No fair, Pete!" Fudge shouted. "He asked me, not you."

"Thank you, Peter," Dad said, and he and Mom shared a look.

"I told you, didn't I?" I said to them. "I told you we have a big problem."

"What problem?" Fudge asked.

"You!" I said.

"Foo!" Tootsie said from her high chair, as she threw a handful of rice across the table.

"What's the difference between dollars and bucks?" Fudge asked the next morning at breakfast. He was drawing dollar signs all over a Cheerios box with a red marker.

"Bucks is just another word for dollars," Mom told him, moving the cereal box out of his reach.

"Nobody says bucks any more," I said. "Where'd you hear about bucks?"

"Grandma was reading me a story and the guy called his money bucks," Fudge said. "He had five bucks and he thought that was a lot. Is that funny or what?" He shovelled a handful of dry Cheerios into his mouth, then washed them down with a swig of milk. He refuses to mix his cereal and milk in a bowl like everyone else.

"Five dollars is nothing to sneeze at," Dad said, carrying

41

Tootsie into the kitchen. "I remember saving for a model aeroplane that cost four dollars and ninety-nine cents, and in those days that *was* a lot." Dad sat Tootsie in her high chair and doled out some Cheerios for her. "Somebody's been decorating the cereal box," he said.

"Yeah, the miser's learned to draw dollar signs," I said.

It wasn't long before the miser started making his own money. "Fudge Bucks," he told us. "I'm going to make a hundred million trillion of them." And just like that, with one box of markers and a pack of coloured paper, he was on his way. "Soon I'll have enough Fudge Bucks to buy the whole world."

"Why don't you start with something smaller," I suggested. "You don't want to buy the whole world right off because then you won't have anything to look forward to."

"Good idea, Pete. I'll start with Toys 'R' Us."

"The kid has no values," I told my parents after Fudge went to bed. They looked at me like I was some kind of crazy. "Well, he doesn't," I said. "He worships money."

"I wouldn't go that far," Dad said. "It's not unusual for young children to want things."

"I want things, too," I reminded Dad. "But I don't go around obsessing about money."

"It's just a phase," Mom said this time.

We could hear Fudge as he started to sing, "*Oh, money, money, money, I love money, money, money . . .*"

As soon as he stopped, Uncle Feather, his myna bird, started. "Ooooo, money, money, money . . ."

Turtle, my dog, lifted his head and howled. He thinks he can sing.

Dad called, "Fudge, cover Uncle Feather's cage and get to sleep."

"Uncle Feather's *mising* his money," Fudge called back. "He's not ready to go to sleep."

"How did this happen to us?" Mom asked. "We've always worked hard. We spend carefully. And we never talk about money in front of the children."

"Maybe that's the problem," I told them.

It was Grandma's idea to take Fudge to Washington, D.C., to the Bureau of Printing and Engraving. "Let him see the green stuff hot off the press," she said to Dad, while the two of them were doing the dinner dishes.

"What green stuff?" Fudge asked. They thought he was safely tucked away in bed but I'd seen him crawl under the kitchen table, where he was listening to every word.

"Fudge, what are you doing under the table?" Mom asked on her way back from putting Tootsie to sleep. "You're supposed to be in bed."

"I can't go to bed until I know about the green stuff."

"What green stuff?" Mom asked.

"I don't know," Fudge said. "That's what I'm trying to find out."

"The green stuff is money," Grandma explained.

"Oh, money," Fudge said. "I *love* money!"

"We know," I told him.

"Are you going to cook some money?" he asked Grandma, laughing.

Grandma laughed with him and shook her head. "You don't *cook* it. The government *prints* it."

"I can print," Fudge said. "I can print the whole alphabet."

"We *know*," I said.

"Fudge," Mom said, "come out from under the table right now. Otherwise we won't have time for a story."

"I want Grandma to read tonight."

"I'd be honoured," she told him.

"Will you read me a story about the green stuff?"

"I'm not sure you have any books about the green stuff," Grandma said. "But maybe I can make up a story about a little boy who liked money so much –"

"So much what?" Fudge asked. "So much he ate it?"

"You'll find out when you're in bed and I tell you the *whole* story," Grandma said. From the way she pressed her lips together, I could tell she was wondering how she was going to get out of this one.

The next morning Grandma reported that Fudge had been

engrossed by her story about a boy who went to Washington to learn how money was made. Mom and Dad took that as an omen.

"A trip certainly couldn't hurt," Mom said. "Remember when you took me on that tour?" she asked Grandma.

"Yes, I do," Grandma said.

"It might even help Fudge understand," Dad agreed. "Good idea, Muriel!"

Grandma beamed.

"We haven't been to Washington in ages," Mom said.

"I've *never* been there," I told them. "Jimmy Fargo says the Air and Space Museum is so cool. Can we check it out?"

"Sounds good to me," Dad said.

Grandma volunteered to stay at our apartment with Tootsie, Turtle and Uncle Feather. And a week later, when school was closed for two days because of teachers' meetings, we headed for Washington, D.C.

We started out early and ate breakfast on the train. Fudge was really impressed by the buffet car. As soon as we carried our food to our seats, he was ready to go back for more. Mom and Dad were sitting in the row in front of us, so I was the one who he kept annoying. "Come on, Pete, let's go back to the buffet car."

"I'm still eating," I told him, slurping up the last of my juice.

He was quiet for about two minutes. Then he asked. "Are we almost there, Pete?"

"No, we're not almost there. We're not even close. It takes three hours to get to Washington, so why don't you look at your books, or draw a picture or something."

I got out my Electroman Advanced Plus. But just as I started a game Fudge covered the screen with his hand. "Will you take me back to the buffet car now?"

"If I do, will you leave me alone?"

"Sure, Pete."

I asked Dad for money. He reminded me not to get Fudge any candy, as if I needed reminding. He was already flying high. "A banana would be good," Dad said. "And juice, not soda."

The buffet car was three cars forward. Fudge had already

learned to open the doors between the cars by kicking the *open door* plate at the bottom of each door. He liked the whoosh of air as he raced from car to car. "This is so fun, Pete! I wish we could ride the train every day."

"We ride the subway," I reminded him.

"But there's no buffet car on the subway and the seats aren't soft and when you look out the window it's all dark."

"That's because the subway is an underground train."

"Wow, Pete, I never knew that!"

"Well, now you know."

"William says, *learn something new every day.*"

I snorted.

"William is smart, Pete. He's the smartest teacher in the world."

Sure he is, I thought.

Fudge got a banana and a juice box at the buffet car. While I paid, Fudge peeled all the skin off his banana and shoved half of it into his mouth. His cheeks puffed out and he couldn't talk his mouth was so full. He insisted on carrying the little cardboard box that held the rest of his banana and his juice box. But on the way back from the buffet car the train swerved and Fudge lost his balance. He flew into the lap of a woman in a red suit and coughed out the gooey, half-chewed banana all over her clothes.

"Get off me!" she shouted "Someone get him off me!" She shoved Fudge off her lap as if he were a slobbering dog, or worse. "Ohhh," she cried, "look what you've done. You've ruined my suit." She turned to the man across the aisle. "Can you believe this? And I've got an appointment at the White House!" Then she glared at Fudge, who was picking himself up off the floor. "You know who lives at the White House?" she asked him.

"The President," Fudge said.

"That's right! And I'm going to tell him exactly how I got these stains on my suit." She jumped up and marched to the rear of the car, where there was a rest room.

"Tell him it was a banana," Fudge called. "And tell him my name, too. It's Farley Drexel Hatcher, but he can call me Fudge."

I grabbed him and pulled him back to our seats. No way was I ever taking him to the buffet car again.

When we finally got to Washington our first stop was a tour of the Bureau of Printing and Engraving. That's where the green stuff is printed. There were about twenty other people in our group. Our tour guide's name was Rosie. She had dark eyes, reddish hair and big teeth.

Before our official tour began, Rosie told us some of what we'd see during our tour. *Fun Facts*, she called them. I decided to write her Fun Facts in my notebook in case any of my teachers ever assigned a report on US currency.

"Fun Fact Number One," Rosie said. "The Bureau of Printing and Engraving produces thirty-seven million notes a day, worth about $696 million."

Fudge raised his hand and asked, "Are notes the same as bucks?"

Rosie told him they were. "They're called bills, dollars, bucks –"

Some guy shouted out, "How about moola?" A couple of people laughed. A few more groaned.

"Well, yes," Rosie said. "I suppose some people refer to money as moola or even as dough."

"How about green stuff?" Fudge shouted. "That's what my grandma calls it."

This time almost everyone in our group laughed. Any minute I thought Fudge would take a bow. But Rosie kept checking her watch and asked the group to hold their questions and comments until she was finished running through all her Fun Facts. Then she led us through the metal detector. Fudge asked if we were getting on a plane. Rosie explained that we weren't, but because this is a federal building they had to make sure no one was carrying a weapon.

"A weapon?" Fudge said, right before Dad set off the alarm. Nobody would have paid any attention except that Fudge shouted, "Dad! Are you carrying a weapon?" That got everyone's attention.

"It's his belt buckle, Turkey Brain," I said.

Rosie took a deep breath and checked her watch a couple of times. She was still smiling but she didn't look that happy. She led us down a long hallway. We followed her single file through narrow corridors that twisted and turned. The old wooden floor squeaked under us. Every few minutes we'd stop in front of glass walls that looked down into rooms where we could see the green stuff in production. As the crowd pressed forward to the window wall, Fudge worked his way up front, wedging himself between people's legs if he had to, to get a better view. Then he waved to the workers in the rooms below. I heard him singing under his breath, *"Oh, money, money, money, I love money, money, money . . ."*

I couldn't believe my parents thought bringing him here was a good idea.

We saw the green stuff as it was printed, cut, stacked and counted. Towards the end of the tour Rosie invited Fudge to walk with her since he was so interested. "I love money!" he told her.

"Well, you've come to the right place," Rosie said.

"Want to see mine?" He pulled out a jumble of Fudge Bucks. "I make it myself. Pretty good, huh?"

"Play money is fine," Rosie told him, "as long as you don't try to use it or pass it off as real because then you could get in big trouble."

"Why?" Fudge said.

"Because that's the rule," Rosie said, firmly, which shut him up until the end of the tour. That's when Rosie asked our group if anyone had any special questions. Fudge's hand shot up first. Rosie didn't look thrilled but she had no choice. She had to call on him.

"I still need to find out how you get a lot of it all at once," Fudge said.

"A lot of . . ." Rosie sounded confused.

"Money!" Fudge shouted.

Mom stepped in and tried to explain. "Fudge has become very curious about money," she told Rosie. "And we thought that by bringing him here . . ."

"I hear what you're saying," Rosie said to Mom. "But somebody has to set him straight."

"I'll set him straight," a tall man with silver hair said. "First of all, young man, you need to get a good education. Then, when you're grown up, you need a good job. Then you save something from your salary every week. You invest carefully. You let your money work for you. And by the time you're my age, with luck, you'll have a nice little nest egg for your retirement."

Our group applauded.

But Fudge still wasn't satisfied. "Or else someone can just give it to you," he said.

You could hear the tongues clucking and the whispers in the crowd. I heard someone say, "This kid is hopeless."

That's when Rosie announced that the next tour was about to begin and we could all proceed to the gift shop. "You're going to love the gift shop," she told Fudge. "All the children do."

"Gift shop?" Mom said. "Warren, did you know there was a gift shop?"

Dad groaned.

WUNDERPANTS

PAUL JENNINGS

MY DAD IS NOT A BAD SORT OF BLOKE. There are plenty who are much worse. But he does rave on a bit, like if you get muddy when you are catching frogs, or rip your jeans when you are building a tree hut. Stuff like that.

Mostly we understand each other and I can handle him. What he doesn't know doesn't hurt him. If he knew that I kept Snot, my pet rabbit, under the bed, he wouldn't like it; so I don't tell him. That way he is happy, I am happy and Snot is happy.

There are only problems when he finds out what has been going on. Like the time that I wanted to see *Mad Max II*. The old man said it was a bad movie – too much blood and guts.

"It's too violent," he said.

"But, Dad, that's not fair. All the other kids are going. I'll be the only one in the school who hasn't seen it." I went on and on like this. I kept nagging. In the end he gave in – he wasn't a bad old boy. He usually let me have what I wanted after a while. It was easy to get around him.

The trouble started the next morning. He was cleaning his teeth in the bathroom, making noises, humming and gurgling – you know the sort of thing. Suddenly he stopped. Everything went quiet. Then he came into the kitchen. There was toothpaste all around his mouth; he looked like a mad tiger. He was frothing at the mouth.

"What's this?" he said. He was waving his toothbrush about. "What's this on my toothbrush?" Little grey hairs were sticking out of it. "How did these hairs get on my toothbrush? Did you have my toothbrush, David?"

He was starting to get mad. I didn't know whether to own up or not. Parents always tell you that if you own up they will let you off. They say that they won't do anything if you are honest – no punishment.

I decided to give it a try. "Yes," I said. "I used it yesterday."

He still had toothpaste on his mouth. He couldn't talk properly. "What are these little grey hairs?" he asked.

"I used it to brush my pet mouse," I answered.

"Your what?" he screamed.

"My mouse."

He started jumping up and down and screaming. He ran around in circles holding his throat, then he ran into the bathroom and started washing his mouth out. There was a lot of splashing and gurgling. He was acting like a madman.

I didn't know what all the fuss was about. All that yelling just over a few mouse hairs.

After a while he came back into the kitchen. He kept opening and shutting his mouth as if he could taste something bad. He had a mean look in his eye – real mean.

"What are you thinking of?" he yelled at the top of his voice. "Are you crazy or something? Are you trying to kill me? Don't you know that mice carry germs? They are filthy things. I'll probably die of some terrible disease."

He went on and on like this for ages. Then he said, "And don't think that you are going to see *Mad Max II*. You can sit at home and think how stupid it is to brush a mouse with someone else's toothbrush."

I went back to my room to get dressed. Dad just didn't understand about that mouse. It was a special mouse, a very special mouse indeed. It was going to make me a lot of money:

fifty dollars, in fact. Every year there was a mouse race in Smith's barn. The prize was fifty dollars. And my mouse, Swift Sam, had a good chance of winning. But I had to look after him. That's why I brushed him with a toothbrush.

I knew that Swift Sam could beat every other mouse except one. There was one mouse I wasn't sure about. It was called Mugger and it was owned by Scrag Murphy, the toughest kid in the town. I had never seen his mouse, but I knew it was fast. Scrag Murphy fed it on a special diet.

That is what I was thinking about as I dressed. I went over to the cupboard to get a pair of underpants. There were none there. "Hey, Mum," I yelled out. "I am out of underpants."

Mum came into the room holding something terrible. Horrible. It was a pair of home-made underpants. "I made these for you, David," she said. "I bought the material at the Op Shop. There was just the right amount of material for one pair of underpants."

"I'm not wearing those," I told her. "No way. Never."

"What's wrong with them?" said Mum. She sounded hurt.

"They're pink," I said. "And they've got little pictures of fairies on them. I couldn't wear them. Everyone would laugh. I would be the laughing stock of the school."

Underpants with fairies on them and pink. I nearly freaked out. I thought about what Scrag Murphy would say if he ever heard about them. I went red just thinking about it.

Just then Dad poked his head into the room. He still had that mean look in his eye. He was remembering the toothbrush. "What's going on now?" he asked in a black voice.

"Nothing," I said. "I was just thanking Mum for making me these nice underpants." I pulled on the fairy pants and quickly covered them up with my jeans. At least no one would know I had them on. That was one thing to be thankful for.

The underpants felt strange. They made me tingle all over. And my head felt light. There was something not quite right about those underpants – and I am not talking about the fairies.

I had breakfast and went to the front gate. Pete was waiting for me.

He is my best mate; we always walk to school together. "Have you got your running shoes?" he asked.

"Oh no," I groaned. "I forgot. It's the cross-country race today." I went back and got my running shoes. I came back out walking very slowly. I was thinking about the race. I would have to go to the changing rooms and get changed in front of Scrag Murphy and all the other boys. They would all laugh their heads off when they saw my fairy underpants.

We walked through the park on the way to school. There was a big lake in the middle. "Let's chuck some stones," said Pete. "See who can throw the furthest." I didn't even answer. I was feeling weak in the stomach. "What's the matter with you?" he asked. "You look like death warmed up."

I looked around. There was no one else in the park. "Look at this," I said. I undid my fly and showed Pete the underpants. His eyes bugged out like organ stops; then he started to laugh. He fell over on the grass and laughed his silly head off. Tears rolled down his cheeks. He really thought it was funny. Some friend.

After a while Pete stopped laughing. "You poor thing," he said. "What are you going to do? Scrag Murphy and the others will never let you forget it."

We started throwing stones into the lake. I didn't try very hard. My heart wasn't in it. "Hey," said Pete. "That was a good shot. It went right over to the other side." He was right. The stone had reached the other side of the lake. No one had ever done that before; it was too far.

I picked up another stone. This time I threw it as hard as I could. The stone went right over the lake and disappeared over some trees. "Wow," yelled Pete. "That's the best shot I've ever seen. No one can throw that far." He looked at me in a funny way.

My skin was all tingling. "I feel strong," I said. "I feel as if I can do anything." I went over to a park bench. It was a large concrete one. I lifted it up with one hand. I held it high over my head. I couldn't believe it.

Pete just stood there with his mouth hanging open. He couldn't believe it either. I felt great. I jumped for joy. I sailed into the air. I went up three metres. "What a jump," yelled Pete.

My skin was still tingling. Especially under the underpants. "It's the underpants," I said. "The underpants are giving me strength." I grinned. "They are not underpants. They are wunderpants."

"SuperJocks," said Pete. We both started cackling like a couple of hens. We laughed until our sides ached.

I told Pete not to tell anyone about the wunderpants. We decided to keep it a secret. Nothing much happened until the cross country race that afternoon. All the boys went to the changing room to put on their running gear. Scrag Murphy was there. I tried to get into my shorts without him seeing my wunderpants, but it was no good. He noticed them as soon as I dropped my jeans.

"Ah ha," he shouted. "Look at baby britches. Look at his fairy pants." Everyone looked. They all started to laugh. How embarrassing. They were all looking at the fairies on my wunderpants.

Scrag Murphy was a big, fat bloke. He was really tough. He came over and pulled the elastic on my wunderpants. Then he let it go. "Ouch," I said. "Cut that out. That hurts."

"What's the matter, little Diddums?" he said. "Can't you take it?" He shoved me roughly against the wall. I wasn't going to let him get away with that, so I pushed him back – just a little push. He went flying across the room and crashed into the wall on the other side. I just didn't know my own strength. That little push had sent him all that way. It was the wunderpants.

Scrag Murphy looked at me with shock and surprise that soon turned to a look of hate. But he didn't say anything. No one said anything. They were all thinking I was going to get my block knocked off next time I saw Scrag Murphy.

About forty kids were running in the race. We had to run through the countryside, following markers that had been put out by the teachers. It was a hot day, so I decided to wear a pair of shorts but no top.

As soon as the starting gun went I was off like a flash. I had kept my wunderpants on and they were really working well.

I went straight out to the front. I had never run so fast before. As I ran along the road I passed a man on a bike. He tried to keep up with me, but he couldn't. Then I passed a car. This was really something. This was great.

I looked behind. None of the others were in sight – I was miles ahead. The trail turned off the road and into the bush. I was running along a narrow track in the forest. After a while I came to a small creek. I was hot so I decided to have a dip. After all, the others were a long way behind; I had plenty of time. I took off my shorts and running shoes, but I left the wunderpants on. I wasn't going to part with them.

I dived into the cold water. It was refreshing. I lay on my back looking at the sky. Life was good. These wunderpants were terrific. I would never be scared of Scrag Murphy while I had them on.

Then something started to happen – something terrible. The wunderpants started to get tight. They hurt. They were shrinking. They were shrinking smaller and smaller. The pain was awful. I had to get them off. I struggled and wriggled; they were so tight they cut into my skin. In the end I got them off, and only just in time. They shrank so small that they would only just fit over my thumb. I had a narrow escape. I could have been killed by the shrinking wunderpants.

Just then I heard voices coming. It was the others in the race. I was trapped – I couldn't get out to put on my shorts. There were girls in the race. I had to stay in the middle of the creek in the nude.

It took quite a while for all the others to run by. They were all spread out along the track. Every time I went to get out of the pool, someone else would come. After a while Pete stopped at the pool. "What are you doing?" he said. "Even superjocks won't help you win from this far back."

"Keep going," I said. "I'll tell you about it later." I didn't want to tell him that I was in the nude. Some girls were with him.

Pete and the girls took off along the track. A bit later the last runner arrived. It was Scrag Murphy. He couldn't run fast – he was carrying too much weight. "Well, look at this," he said.

"It's little Fairy Pants. And what's this we have here?" he picked up my shorts and running shoes from the bank of the creek. Then he ran off with them.

"Come back," I screamed. "Bring those back here." He didn't take any notice. He just laughed and kept running.

I didn't know what to do. I didn't have a stitch of clothing. I didn't even have any shoes. I was starting to feel cold; the water was freezing. I was covered in goose pimples and my teeth were chattering. In the end I had to get out. I would have frozen to death if I stayed in the water any longer.

I went and sat on a rock in the sun and tried to think of a way to get home without being seen. It was all right in the bush. I could always hide behind a tree if someone came. But once I reached the road I would be in trouble; I couldn't just walk along the road in the nude.

Then I had an idea. I looked at the tiny underpants. I couldn't put them on, but they still might work. I put them over my thumb and jumped. It was no good. It was just an ordinary small jump. I picked up a stone and threw it. It only went a short way, not much of a throw at all. The pants were too small, and I was my weak old self again.

I lay down on the rock in the sun. Ants started to crawl over me. Then the sun went behind a cloud. I started to get cold, but I couldn't walk home – not in the raw. I felt miserable. I looked around for something to wear, but there was nothing. Just trees, bushes and grass.

I knew I would have to wait until dark. The others would all have gone home by now. Pete would think I had gone home, and my parents would think I was at his place. No one was going to come and help me.

I started to think about Scrag Murphy. He was going to pay for this. I would get him back somehow.

Time went slowly, but at last it started to grow dark. I made my way back along the track. I was in bare feet and I kept standing on stones. Branches reached out and scratched me in all sorts of painful places. Then I started to think about snakes. What if I stood on one?

There were all sorts of noises in the dark. The moon had gone in, and it was hard to see where I was going. I have to admit it: I was scared. Scared stiff. To cheer myself up I started to think about what I was going to do to Scrag Murphy. Boy, was he going to get it.

At last I came to the road. I was glad to be out of the bush. My feet were cut and bleeding and I hobbled along. Every time a car went by I had to dive into the bushes. I couldn't let myself get caught in the headlights of the cars.

I wondered what I was going to do when I reached the town. There might be people around. I broke off a branch from a bush and held it in front of my "you know what". It was prickly, but it was better than nothing.

By the time I reached the town it was late. There was no one around. But I had to be careful – someone might come out of a house at any minute. I ran from tree to tree and wall to wall, hiding in the shadows as I went. Lucky for me the moon was in and it was very dark.

Then I saw something that gave me an idea – a phone box. I opened the door and stepped inside. A dim light shone on my naked body. I hoped that no one was looking. I had no money, but Pete had told me that if you yell into the earpiece they can hear you on the other end. It was worth a try. I dialled our home number. Dad answered. "Yes," he said.

"I'm in the nude," I shouted. "I've lost my clothes. Help. Help."

"Hello, hello. Who's there?" said Dad.

I shouted at the top of my voice, but Dad just kept saying "Hello". He sounded cross. Then I heard him say to Mum, "It's probably that boy up to his tricks again." He hung up the phone.

I decided to make a run for it. It was the only way. I dropped my bush and started running. I went for my life. I reached our street without meeting a soul. I thought I was safe, but I was wrong. I crashed right into someone and sent them flying. It was old Mrs Jeeves from across the road.

"Sorry," I said. "Gee, I'm sorry." I helped her stand up. She was a bit short sighted and it was dark. She hadn't noticed that

I didn't have any clothes on. Then the moon came out – the blazing moon. I tried to cover my nakedness with my hands, but it was no good.

"Disgusting," she screeched. "Disgusting. I'll tell your father about this."

I ran home as fast as I could. I went in the back door and jumped into bed. I tried to pretend that I was asleep. Downstairs I could hear Mrs Jeeves yelling at Dad; then the front door closed. I heard his footsteps coming up the stairs.

Well, I really copped it. I was in big trouble. Dad went on and on. "What are you thinking of, lad? Running around in the nude. Losing all your clothes. What will the neighbours think?" He went on like that for about a week. I couldn't tell him the truth – he wouldn't believe it. No one would. The only ones who knew the whole story were Pete and I.

Dad grounded me for a month. I wasn't allowed out of the house except to go to school. No pictures, no swimming, nothing. And no pocket money either.

It was a bad month. Very bad indeed. At school Scrag Murphy gave me a hard time. He called me "Fairy Pants". Everyone thought it was a great joke, and there was nothing I could do about it. He was just too big for me, and his mates were all tough guys.

"This is serious," said Pete. "We have to put Scrag Murphy back in his box. They are starting to call me 'Friend of Fairy Pants' now. We have to get even."

We thought and thought but we couldn't come up with anything. Then I remembered the mouse race in Smith's barn. "We will win the mouse race," I shouted. "It's in a month's time. We can use the next month to train my mouse."

"That's it," said Pete. "The prize is fifty dollars. Scrag Murphy thinks he is going to win. It will really get up his nose if we take off the prize."

I went and fetched Swift Sam. "He's small," I said. "But he's fast. I bet he can beat Murphy's mouse. It's called Mugger."

We started to train Swift Sam. Every day after school we took him around a track in the back yard. We tied a piece of cheese on the end of a bit of string. Swift Sam chased after it as fast as he could. After six laps we gave him a piece of cheese to eat. At the start he could do six laps in ten minutes. By the end of the month he was down to three minutes.

"Scrag Murphy, look out," said Pete with a grin. "We are really going to beat the pants off you this time."

The day of the big race came at last. There were about one hundred kids in Smith's barn. No adults knew about it – they would probably have stopped it if they knew. It cost fifty cents to get in. That's where the prize money came from. A kid called Tiger Gleeson took up the money and gave out the prize at the end. He was the organizer of the whole thing.

Scrag Murphy was there, of course. "It's in the bag," he swaggered. "Mugger can't lose. I've fed him on a special diet. He is the fittest mouse in the county. He will eat Swift Sam, just you wait and see."

I didn't say anything. But I was very keen to see his mouse, Mugger. Scrag Murphy had it in a box. No one had seen it yet.

"Right," said Tiger. "Get out your mice." I put Swift Sam down on the track. He looked very small. He started sniffing around. I hoped he would run as fast with the other mice there – he hadn't had any match practice before. Then the others put their mice on the track. Everyone except Scrag Murphy. He still had Mugger in the box.

Scrag Murphy put his hand in the box and took out Mugger. He was the biggest mouse I had ever seen. He was at least ten times as big as Swift Sam. "Hey," said Pete. "That's not a mouse. That's a rat. You can't race a rat. It's not fair."

"It's not a rat," said Scrag Murphy in a threatening voice. "It's just a big mouse. I've been feeding it up." I looked at it again. It was a rat all right. It was starting to attack the mice.

"We will take a vote," said Tiger. "All those that think it is a rat, put your hands up." He counted all the hands.

"Fifty," he said. "Now all those who say that Mugger is a mouse put your hands up." He counted again.

"Fifty-two. Mugger is a mouse."

Scrag Murphy and his gang started to cheer. He had brought all his mates with him. It was a put-up job.

"Right," said Tiger Gleeson. "Get ready to race."

There were about ten mice in the race – or I should say nine mice and one rat. Two rats if you counted Scrag Murphy. All the owners took out their string and cheese. "Go," shouted Tiger Gleeson.

Mugger jumped straight onto a little mouse next to him and bit it on the neck. The poor thing fell over and lay still. "Boo," yelled some of the crowd.

Swift Sam ran to the front straight away. He was going really well. Then Mugger started to catch up. It was neck and neck for five laps. First Mugger would get in front, then Swift Sam. Everyone in the barn went crazy. They were yelling their heads off.

By the sixth lap Mugger started to fall behind. All the other mice were not in the race. They had been lapped twice by Mugger and Swift Sam. But Mugger couldn't keep up with Swift Sam; he was about a tail behind. Suddenly something terrible happened. Mugger jumped onto Swift Sam's tail and grabbed it in his teeth. The crowd started to boo. Even Scrag Murphy's mates were booing.

But Swift Sam kept going. He didn't stop for a second. He just pulled that great rat along after him. It rolled over and over behind the little mouse. Mugger held on for grim death, but he couldn't stop Swift Sam. "What a mouse," screamed the crowd as Swift Sam crossed the finish line still towing Mugger behind him.

Scrag Murphy stormed off out of the barn. He didn't even take Mugger with him. Tiger handed me the fifty dollars. Then he held up Swift Sam. "Swift Sam is the winner," he said. "The only mouse in the world with its own little pair of fairy underpants."

A WORK OF ART

MARGARET MAHY

MRS BASKIN'S BIG SON, Brian, was working in another city, but he was coming home for his birthday, so she decided to make him a rich fruitcake and to ice it herself. She had been taking cake-icing lessons at the Polytechnic for nearly a year and by now she felt she was rather good at it, better indeed than her instructor, who liked brightly coloured, frilly sort of icing. Mrs Baskin preferred something plainer and cooler. As she got out the cake mixing bowl, wooden spoon, a big plastic bowl for the dried fruit, the sifter for sifting the dry ingredients, as well as the big, hinged cake-tin, a picture came into her mind of how the cake might look: pure, almost – but not quite – unearthly, a cake that had been iced by moonlight on midsummer night. She looked at her calendar and saw with pleasure that it would be full moon that night.

Mrs Baskin set about things in a very orderly fashion. First she greased one side of the greaseproof paper with a knob of butter, and then she fitted it, butterside up, in the big, hinged cake-tin. She turned on the oven so that it would be heating while she worked. Then she put the dried fruit into the plastic bowl – currants, candied peel, sultanas, seedless raisins, a little bit of chopped ginger and almonds, as well as glacé cherries and crystallized angelica to give a bit of colour to the cake when it was sliced. Once she'd mixed the dried fruit, she floured it a little so the fruit wouldn't stick to itself. Then she sifted half a pound of plain flour and half a teaspoon of baking powder into yet another bowl, an old pottery one that had belonged to her mother.

Her three youngest children, Hamlet, Serena and Toby, watched her, for they were as interested in Brian's cake as if it if were theirs too. They were certain Brian would let them have some of it. Even Wellington, the dog, watched, wagging his tail whenever anyone spoke to him. Hubert, the cat, pretended to be asleep, but if you looked closely you could see two thin, green slits in his black face. He liked to know just what was going on in his house.

Mrs Baskin creamed butter and brown sugar until the mixture was light and fluffy, and then beat in four eggs, one at a time. She slowly added the flour, stirring as she went, and finally the fruit mixture. Her arm grew rather tired. Hamlet had a go, but he could scarcely move the spoon. Serena had a go, but she couldn't move it at all. Toby was too little even to try. He could barely stand, let alone stir a birthday cake. Not only that, he was teething and Mrs Baskin thought he might dribble into the mixture. Of course, Wellington and Hubert were no use at all.

Just then, the big girls, Audrey and Vanilla, came in from school, arguing and hitting each other with their school bags. But they stopped fighting when they saw that their mother was making a birthday cake. They quickly realized that there would be delicious cake mixture left on the inside of the mixing bowl.

"Mum, Mum, can I lick the bowl?" they cried together.

There was an immediate rush for the spoon drawer. Everyone but Toby grabbed a spoon. Mrs Baskin carefully scraped most of the mixture into her hinged cake-tin and put it in the oven.

At that moment one of the middle boys, Leonard, came in from cricket practice. Mrs Baskin gave him the mixing spoon to lick. Audrey said it wasn't fair. Vanilla said Serena was letting her hair drag in the bowl. Serena hit Hamlet with her spoon for taking too much. Hamlet pretended he was badly hurt, fell over backwards and knocked Toby over. Immediately, Wellington stood on everyone and began licking the bowl before anyone else.

After she had baked the cake for an hour and a half, Mrs Baskin lowered the oven temperature and baked it for a further two and a quarter hours. By the time it was ready to come out of the tin the other middle boy, Greville, came in. The bowl and the mixing spoon were washed and put away by then, but Greville didn't care. He had had a secret meal of fish and chips with his friend Simon, under Simon's bed. He liked the look of the cake though, and said he couldn't wait for Brian to get home.

When the cake was properly cool, Mrs Baskin brushed it with apricot glaze before covering it with almond paste. Then she drove Greville away from the television (the six youngest children were already in bed), made herself a cup of tea, turned the television off, and sat in the moony dark for a little while, getting herself into a magic, cake-icing mood. She had a short, refreshing sleep, then got up, washed her face and put on some make-up (so as to get in a birthday party mood). She thought about Brian who had been her first baby. She thought about him growing year by year, losing teeth, scraping his knees, learning how to ride a bike, going to college, and so on. The cake needed to be iced in such a way that anyone who saw it would somehow be aware of these things. She would not write *Happy Birthday* on it but she would ice it so that anyone who saw it would *feel* Happy Birthday-ish.

While she iced, the moon peered in at the window, looking rather like an iced cake itself. Mrs Baskin smiled and waved to it. She thought it looked surprised but pleased. When she had finished icing the cake she put it on a silver stand and then, because it seemed a pity to shut it away in a cake-tin, she covered it with a glass dome which had once belonged to her grandmother, and stood it on top of the piano. The moon looked in and touched it gently. The cake seemed to glow with a moony light of its own.

When the children saw the cake next morning they all stood and stared at it, astonished.

"Gee, Mum, it's too good to eat," said Greville, though he didn't really mean it.

The children who were old enough to go to school went to school; the little children played under the table. Mrs Baskin began to vacuum the house. The vacuum cleaner made a lot of noise and she did not hear the knock at the door, but Hamlet heard it. He opened the door and let two men in. One was dressed in a floppy, striped shirt and designer-jeans. The other wore an elegant suit.

"Excuse us," they said, "but we are the owners of the art gallery down the road. We just happened to be passing and we saw that wonderful thing you have there on your piano. Is it yours?"

Mrs Baskin explained that it was hers in a way. She had made it. However, the real owner was her son, Brian, who would be coming home in a month's time.

"It's a very rich cake," she explained, "and it will improve over the next month. Cakes like these improve with keeping."

The gallery owners, who were both on permanent diets, did not know much about cakes. They were astonished to find the elegant sculpture they had admired through the window was actually an iced birthday cake.

"It has a certain look, a certain ambience . . . I don't know! What would you say, Wynstan?" asked the one in the striped, floppy shirt, whose own name was Zachary.

"Purity!" said Wynstan. "What do you say, Zack? Shall we make an offer?"

They offered Mrs Baskin fifty dollars for her cake. She was certainly tempted. But it would not be full moon again for a month, and she had iced that cake at that special time in that special way for Brian. If she sold it she knew she could not make another one quite as good until it was full moon again.

"I'll rent it to you for fifty dollars," she said at last. "But you must get it insured against anyone eating it and you mustn't take it from under the glass dome or it'll get dusty."

She didn't think they would take her up on her offer but, after a lot of frowning and arguing, they did. There was something about that cake – they couldn't quite say what it was – but they were determined to display it in their gallery. They came round with a van later in the day and carried it off.

When the little ones saw the cake being carried off, they all began to cry. Mrs Baskin told them that it would be coming back again but they did not believe her. They were sure the gallery owners would take the cake into their gallery and eat it all themselves. Being so small they didn't understand that it was insured.

The next morning on the front page of the newspaper, there was a photograph of Mrs Baskin's cake. *Tour de force by Local Artist*, said a headline.

"It's not a *tour de force*," complained Audrey. "It's an iced cake."

"Gee, you're dumb," said Greville. "A *tour de force* means a – it means something terrific."

"You don't know what it means either!" said Vanilla, who always stuck up for Audrey when Audrey was arguing with Greville. Greville went into his room pretending he didn't care, and looked up *tour de force* in the dictionary.

"*Tour de force* means feat of strength or skill, you noddy!" he said when he came back.

"Mum, Greville's calling me a noddy!" complained Audrey.

"That means I've got two *tour de forces*," said Leonard, dancing up and down. "Feet of skill and strength."

"Well, they smell pretty strong after you've been playing cricket," said Vanilla.

"That's enough of that," said Mrs Baskin. She had been trying to talk to someone on the phone. "Help me tidy the house! The television people are coming round."

The children were so impressed at the thought of being on television that they raced about helping their mother by turning cushions upside down so that the cat fur Hubert had left on them was underneath. But by half-past eight the cameras had still not arrived and the big children had to go to school.

Mrs Baskin wished she had had time to get her hair set, but it was too late. She tore into the bathroom and put on some lipstick and eyeliner to brighten herself up a bit. The television people came in, Wellington barked himself hoarse, while Hubert panicked and shot up the curtains to hide on top of the bookshelf.

"When did you get the idea of using cake as an art form?" asked the television interviewer. "Is it a feminist protest against being a slave in the kitchen?"

"No, it's a birthday cake," said Mrs Baskin. "My son, Brian, is coming home for his birthday next month and I made a cake for him."

Mrs Baskin was on television that night. Apart from her hair, she thought she did pretty well, but she wasn't the only person on the programme. There was a man from the local university talking about her cake.

"What we see here is a return to folk art . . . to the art of the *people*," he said. "It is functional art – this cake is meant to be *used*, and yet the artist shows instinctive awareness of texture and balance. She *interprets* the quality of *cakeness* and tests her creation against traditional concepts. Tradition is recognized, and yet I think we are witnessing the emergence of a new dynamic."

"Wow, Mum!" said Greville.

"Pretty cool!" said Vanilla. "But when are they going to bring that cake back?"

"Brian doesn't come home for a month," Mrs Baskin said. "That cake's probably safer there than it is here."

"You bet!" agreed Leonard, clashing his knife and fork, which encouraged all the little ones to clash their knives and forks, too.

"Now then," said Mrs Baskin, "that's enough of that! You kids can do the dishes. I'm going out."

"Where are you going?" asked Audrey.

"Just down the road to the gallery," said Mrs Baskin. "Greville will babysit. You can put Toby to bed, Leonard! Read Hamlet a story, Vanilla!"

She put on her best dress and went down to the gallery. Her iced cake looked very beautiful, very mysterious, sitting in the window. It looked a little like a lot of different things, but most of all it looked like something simple which somehow nobody had ever noticed until now. It was the mixture of looking like a lot of other things and looking like something entirely new that made it so astonishing. As well as all that it was a cake. Everyone liked it.

When Mrs Baskin stepped into the gallery, Zack and Wynstan ran to meet her. Zack kissed her right hand and Wynstan kissed her left, and Wynstan's mother came to tell her how thrilling her cake was.

"When I saw it, I said that's *art*! I said, that's what art's about. It's a cake – yes – but not *just* a cake. It's a statement in its own right. My dear, it's got such passionate equilibrium."

Mrs Baskin talked to a lot of interesting people in the gallery, drank some sherry and ate a slice of another, inferior cake. She enjoyed herself and was able to check that her cake was being well looked after. The gallery was dust free and had controlled humidity.

The next day she had her hair set, and it was just as well she did, for two reporters from art magazines came to talk to her, bringing photographers with them.

"I can't tell you how much I admire it," said one reporter. "The stand, the cake itself, and the dome, are all organized to make separate yet identical statements. You've somehow represented the finite universe, continuous in space, powerful in its defiance of causality, but threatened by entropy. And then there's the time dimension. Implicit in it are times we can define as *before cake* and *after cake*.

When they had gone, Mrs Baskin went down to the gallery again. She had to wait in a small queue that had formed in order to look at her cake. People stared through the glass longingly, and it took quite a while for the queue to move. At last it was Mrs Baskin's turn. As she filed past it she took a good hard look at it. She saw that all the things the critics and reporters were saying could be quite true. She saw that the cake was looking as fresh as ever and that there was no dust on it.

Over the next day or two Mrs Baskin received phone calls from London and New York. Certain art galleries were anxious to display her cake. Others were flying art critics over to write about it.

Vanilla and Audrey quickly learned to talk like art critics.

"Audrey, what do you think of the sculptural projection of this sandwich?" Vanilla would ask.

"I think it's visually significant," Audrey would say. "But the tomato's sliding out of it!"

"I made it like that on purpose," Vanilla cried, catching the tomato. "To give it immediacy."

"Gee, what a pair of noddys!" exclaimed Leonard.

"Noddys!" repeated Hamlet, pleased to join in talking to the big ones.

"Mum, Leonard's teaching Hamlet to call us noddys," shouted Audrey and Vanilla together.

Three weeks later it was announced that Mrs Baskin had won a medal for a significant contribution to new art. The President of the Society of Arts presented the medal and shook her hand.

"What a cake!" He cried. "It has a certain Byzantine quality, no?"

"Maybe . . ." said Mrs Baskin. Once people had pointed out things about her cake to her she often saw them herself. Had they been there all the time? Or did people call them into being by naming them? And did it matter?

At the end of a fortnight there was a change of display at the gallery and her cake was sent home.

"But don't worry!" said Wynstan. "We have lots of openings for it. Let us be your agents: your cake has a brilliant career in front of it."

Never had his gallery been so full. Never had there been such queues or such enthusiasm. He and Zack were planning a great pikelet-and-jam exhibition. He could hear the critics now. "There is an effortless virtuosity about the way the jam is applied that takes the breath away," or, "The static alignment of the pikelet brings out the semi-fluid texture of the jam component."

He went home feeling very happy.

His mother had made him a pancake, not great art, but very tasty. Suddenly, the phone rang. Wynstan answered it. Within ten minutes he had leaped into his car and rushed around to get Zack. Within three minutes they were on their way to Mrs Baskin's.

They did not knock. They burst into her front room and found her among her children – Toby, Serena, Hamlet, Audrey, Vanilla, Leonard and Greville. But there was one other. A tall, young man sat there with Hubert on his knees and Wellington under his chair. Everyone had a very well-fed look.

Wynstan seized Mrs Baskin's hand.

"Wonderful news, dear!" he said. "I've just had a Japanese firm on the phone and they want to buy your cake for ten thousand."

"Ten thousand what?" asked Mrs Baskin.

"Dollars, pounds, yen . . . who cares!" cried Zack. "We'll only take fifteen per cent commission and the rest of that lovely lolly will be yours. Where is the cake?"

Mrs Baskin pointed.

What was left of it was in the middle of the table. The cherries and the angelica glowed like rubies and emeralds among the dark, rich crumbs.

"You've eaten it?" cried Wynstan. "You've eaten a work of art."

"We all did," said Brian (for the young man with Hubert on his knee was Brian). "It was my birthday cake!"

"But that wasn't just a cake. It was art!" cried Wynstan.

Mrs Baskin got up from the table.

"It was art," she agreed, "But it was also a cake – Brian's birthday cake. Some art is meant to last and some is meant to be eaten up. Not everything has to be a monument."

"It was terrific cake," said Brian. "Have some?"

Wynstan and Zack looked hungrily at the cake.

"Well, maybe just a crumb," said Zack, accepting a large slice. Later, both he and Wynstan had to admit it was the best-tasting art they had ever come across.

Mrs Baskin watched everyone enjoying the cake and thought of her big, hinged cake-tin, the plastic bowl, the pottery bowl, and the big mixing bowl waiting quietly in the dark cupboard, and a mysterious excitement stirred in her.

"I'll make another cake tomorrow . . . but not a birthday cake. You can't make the same cake twice," she thought to herself, and she glanced at the calendar. Four weeks had gone by surprisingly quickly. Tomorrow night the moon would be full again.

HARRY THE STREET PIGEON

M. L. GREENALL

"TYPICAL! Absolutely typical of human feet! Always flattening your food!" grumbled Harry, as he scraped a squashed chocolate-covered raisin off the pavement with his beak. Harry was a London pigeon and he lived on the bits of food people dropped as they passed by in the street. He flew back up to the gutter which was his home above a sweet shop, and thought crossly about feet.

"It's always the best bits they tread on, too. Flat chips! Flat popcorn! Flat peanuts! Flat raisins!" Raisins were Harry's favourite food, and a rare treat. "It would be nice to have one that wasn't squashed flat for a change. How would humans like it if I trod all over *their* food?"

Just then the morning breeze blew across the gutter, carrying with it all the smells of the street. The breeze was like a newspaper to Harry, and he read it every day for new smells. There were all the usual ones – tomatoes and olives from the pizza takeaway, onions and chips from the burger restaurant, coffee from the supermarket – but there were some different ones, too. Old socks, was it? No, not socks, but a fancy cheese at the delicatessen. There was a strong whiff of flea-powder on that snooty Afghan hound passing by on a lead, and there were fresh tulips in the flower shop. And hang about! Wasn't that cake? Not just any old stuff, but top quality cake with loads of raisins and currants, and chocolate and marzipan. A new cake shop must have opened!

"I'm off to investigate. There may be some crumbs I can pick up before they all get trodden on," thought Harry.

He flew down the street, past the cinema and the supermarket, and the TV rental shop, and the hairdresser's shop where a fat woman sat, looking very silly, with pieces of tinfoil in her hair. The smell of cake was growing stronger all the time.

"This is it!" cried Harry suddenly. "And yet it *can't* be! This is the shop which sells pretty ornaments!" the shop door was wide open, and the most beak-watering smells came from inside. Puzzled, Harry flew onto the shop's broad window ledge for a closer look.

"Blow me down with a feather! Those aren't ornaments, they *are* cakes! But I never realized it before, because this shop door has always been shut so I couldn't smell them."

Written across the window in big gold letters were the words GLORIA GOODBODY'S GATEAUX, but Harry didn't know gâteaux was French for cakes.

He stared through the window admiringly. The centre-piece was a chocolate sponge Noah's Ark with Mr and Mrs Noah standing on deck in yellow anoraks and sou'westers. Mr Noah's long white beard was made from icing sugar, and Mrs Noah had two yellow marzipan plaits peeping out below her sou'wester. Behind the Noahs were pairs of marzipan animals. Brightly-coloured fish played in the blue marzipan waves around the Ark, and a white dove sat on the roof with a green twig in its beak.

Another cake was made like a table laid for a birthday party, complete with white tablecloth, little plates and mugs, tiny chocolate éclairs, and even a cake which was a miniature copy of the birthday cake it stood on. Then there was a chocolate thatched cottage with roses growing round the porch, and a marzipan garden full of sugar flowers. And because it was nearly Easter, there were two straw hats which were so realistic you could almost have walked out the shop wearing one, even though they were made from meringue and pastry and syrupy fruit.

But the cake Harry liked most was the one like a green football pitch with a little black and white football in the centre. "Just the right size for a pigeon," he sighed. "How I'd love to kick it into one of those goals like they do on the telly in the TV rental shop."

A woman came out of the shop with a pink cake box tied with gold ribbon. Harry followed her, hoping she would eat the cake in the street and drop some crumbs, as people did when they came out of takeaways, but she carried the box carefully into a taxi. He examined the pavement for crumbs people might have dropped earlier, but there weren't any. It was most disappointing, and the smell of cake was making Harry so hungry.

Harry's mother had taught him never to go into shops or houses because humans were dangerous. "But I can handle people," he thought, "I'm a street pigeon, aren't I? All you've got to do is watch out for their feet. Why, humans are so stupid they can't even fly!"

He took a few cautious steps into the shop. He'd never trodden anywhere so clean in his life. The shiny pink floor felt nice underfoot, but there wasn't a crumb on it anywhere. Two young women in pink pinafores and frilly caps stood chatting behind the counter. They were too deep in conversation to notice Harry.

"It's bloomin' cold with that door open, Hayley," said one.

"I know, Linda," replied Hayley, "but Mrs Goodbody says we must leave it open so the smell of cakes will attract people into the shop."

"I feel ever so silly wearing vanilla essence behind my ears," said Linda.

"So do I," agreed Hayley, "but Mrs Goodbody says it will whet people's appetites and make them buy her cakes."

"*Gâteaux*, Hayley, we're supposed to call them *gâteaux*."

"Expensive is what I call them," grumbled Hayley. "You'd think she could pay us higher wages, the prices she charges. She'll be back from the hairdresser's soon. She's always getting her hair done. I wonder what colour it will be this time? Remember when she wanted it mauve, and it came out orange?

Linda and Hayley giggled so much they didn't see Harry hop up into the window among the cakes.

Harry looked around him and thought, "If I take a little peck from each cake no-one will ever notice. But first I must have a kick at that football." He stepped onto the green iced cake and kicked the ball as hard as he could. It missed the goal, and caught Mr Noah on the back of his head, sending him toppling overboard into a strawberry-filled heart, where he sank halfway up to his beard in red jam.

"Sorry about that, mate," muttered Harry, wondering where the ball had gone. Then he saw it on top of the meringue of one of the hats. It would be fun to have one more kick, and when Harry landed on the hat he had a nasty surprise. It wasn't smooth and firm like the football pitch, but softer than wet snow, and horribly sticky. His feet went through the meringue and into the lemon filling. He sank down until he could feel the little ball beneath his feet where it had settled firmly on the pastry base, but there was no hope of kicking it out. Harry had never realized food could be so deep. He began to panic, and had quite a struggle to get himself out of the hat; and by then it didn't look like a hat any more.

There was a sponge teddy bear in chocolate sunglasses, sunbathing on its back on a little blue and white striped icing-sugar towel. Harry tried to clean up his sticky feet by wiping them on the bear's tummy, but he scuffed up a lot of crumbs, and the bear looked as if it was moulting. Harry ate some of the crumbs to tidy it up, but the bear only looked worse.

Harry soon discovered that some cakes were firm, and others were slippery and gooey. He had a bad moment sliding down the roof of the thatched cottage. It was made of chocolate-butter icing, and his feet left two deep grooves behind him as he slithered off it. He accidentally pulled away the porch and the rambling roses, before landing on the sugar flowers in the marzipan garden and smearing them all with chocolate. Then he hopped onto the cake like a birthday party table, and left chocolate footprints all over it, after pecking some experimental holes. Sponge again! *Where* were the currants and raisins? He could smell them close by.

Right at the back of the display, he spotted a cake shaped like an igloo, and knew at once. "That's where the currants and raisins are – inside it!"

An eskimo with a harpoon stood at the igloo's entrance. Harry didn't like the look of the harpoon, so he pattered round to the back of the igloo, out of the eskimo's sight. He chipped away some icing, and found cake with as many currants and raisins as any pigeon could wish for. He pecked a hole big enough to get his head inside the igloo, and before he realized it he'd eaten it empty.

"That was lovely!" he sighed. "I don't suppose the eskimo will mind when he finds out I've eaten the inside of his igloo. More room for *him* now. But I'm so full, I must have a snooze before I fly home." He hopped onto an empty cake-stand, and was asleep in no time.

It was peaceful in the shop. Hayley had gone to fetch a tray of freshly-baked Danish pastries and currant buns, and Linda was leaning against the counter, staring through the open door, daydreaming. One moment a shop can be quite empty, and the next it is full of people. That's what happened while Harry slept. A little queue formed. Then a woman came in and walked to the head of it. "You won't mind if I'm served first, will you?" she asked the queue. "But I've left my Porsche on a double yellow line."

Some people said they *did* mind, but she ignored them. "I'll have six Danish pastries, six currant buns, and let me see, what else?" She turned to look at the cakes in the window display, and saw Harry dozing on one leg on the cake-stand. "Oh!" she cried. "I must have that *gorgeous* pigeon cake! It's so lifelike! Has it got currants and raisins inside?"

Harry was a light sleeper. He woke instantly. "How does she know I've got currants and raisins inside me?" He drew himself up, and flapped his wings at the woman indignantly. She screamed. "Oh! It's real! How horrible! I'm terrified of real birds!" And she fainted face-down onto the tray of warm Danish pastries that Hayley had just put on the table next to the counter.

It was then that Mrs Goodbody returned from the hairdresser.

Her hair was raspberry pink and brushed up into big waves, and she strode into the shop looking very large and important in a dress the same colour as her hair. She stopped still suddenly, and demanded: "WHO IS THAT WOMAN ASLEEP ON MY DANISH PASTRIES?"

"I don't know her name," said Hayley, "but she's not asleep. She's fainted. The pigeon done it."

"The pigeon *did* it," corrected Mrs Goodbody.

"That's what I said, Mrs Goodbody. The pigeon done it."

"Pigeon?" boomed Mrs Goodbody. "What pigeon done *what?* I mean –" Then she caught sight of Harry, and anger made her quiver like a raspberry jelly that had been struck with a spoon. "Who let that filthy bird in here?" she gasped.

"It must have flown in," said Hayley. "You told us to leave the door open. You said the smell of baking might get the skinflints round here to open their wallets. You said they were all so stingy –"

Mrs Goodbody's face had turned an ugly red, which clashed with her hair.

"Um. Er, er," she stuttered. "That was just a joke, Hayley."

Some of the customers laughed, and Mrs Goodbody's face went even redder.

"I'm getting that disgusting pigeon out of here. Instantly!" she shouted, and pulled on a pair of the hygienic rubber gloves that Hayley and Linda had to wear when they handled the cakes. She advanced towards Harry with a cake slice in one hand and a pink teacloth in the other.

"Don't hurt it!" said one of the customers.

"Hmmmph!" snorted Mrs Goodbody.

Harry didn't like the look in her eye, nor did he like being called disgusting. He spread his wings wide and flapped them at Mrs Goodbody, hoping to make her faint like the other lady. But Mrs Goodbody didn't faint. She brandished the cake slice menacingly, and snarled, "Just wait till I get my hands on you!"

"Not likely," thought Harry – but in his haste to fly off the cake-stand he tipped it over, and it fell against the empty igloo. The icing broke like a china bowl.

"Oh! You've eaten my igloo!" hissed Mrs Goodbody, and then she saw Mr Noah in the strawberry heart, and the grooves in the thatched-cottage roof, and the footprints on the birthday cake, and the ruined meringue hats. "AND WHERE IS MY FOOTBALL?" she shouted.

Harry hopped onto the deck of the Ark out of Mrs Goodbody's reach, but his wing caught Mrs Noah off balance, and sent her "*plop*" into the strawberry heart beside her husband. They looked quite cosy side by side up to their chests in red jam, but Mrs Goodbody didn't think so.

"My Ark! My gâteaux!" she shrieked. "You horrible, revolting bird! Get out of my shop before I murder you!"

"Don't worry, I'm going," thought Harry, but in his haste, he forgot there was a glass window between him and the street, and he flew straight into it. He fell back onto a pair of meringue Easter bunnies who were holding a fragile meringue basket filled with jammy strawberries. Harry flapped so wildly to get back on his feet that the bunnies and their basket were reduced to a blizzard of meringue crumbs, and most of the strawberries were squashed to a pulp.

The flapping roused the woman who had fainted, and she lifted her head in a daze. "Am I in heaven?" she asked Hayley. "I can hear the beat of angels' wings!"

"No, that's just the pigeon," said Hayley, and the woman fainted back onto the Danish pastries again.

The photographer from the local paper dropped into the shop to buy a currant bun for his elevenses. "Lucky I've got my camera with me," he thought. "Could be a front page picture here. What a mess! That old girl with the raspberry hair looks in a right old temper. I don't fancy the pigeon's chances against *her*."

Mrs Goodbody took a swipe at Harry with the cake slice, and missed. He leapt up in terror and tried to fly over her, but a large strawberry had caught on his claw, and the weight of it forced him to crash-land on her head. Mrs Goodbody wasn't so frightening to Harry now that he couldn't see her angry face. Her hair was still warm from its blow dry, and he found it good for cleaning his sticky feet. He shook the strawberry from

his claw, and it slid through Mrs Goodbody's hair and stuck to her eyebrow. Several people laughed, but they tried to make it sound as though they were coughing.

"My hair! My highlights!" Mrs Goodbody screamed.

"Watch the birdie!" said the photographer from the doorway. Mrs Goodbody made a strangled sound.

"Only joking!" he said, his camera flashing.

"Don't you dare print that photograph!" cried Mrs Goodbody.

"Publicity! Just what you need to send your sales roaring," replied the photographer. "Now give us a smile, darling."

Mrs Goodbody glared.

"Think how light your cakes must be to break so easily," said a customer, encouragingly. "Think of all the lovely trifle you can make with the broken bits," said another. "Think of all the lovely insurance you can claim!" said the photographer. Mrs Goodbody beamed, and the camera flashed again.

Meanwhile Harry had seen the open doorway. He gave his feet one last wipe on Mrs Goodbody's hair, then spread his wings and flew off into the street. The photographer took a final picture of him, and some of the people in the shop cheered Harry on his way.

"That's positively the last time I'm ever eating indoors," thought Harry, as he splashed under the fountain in the square round the corner a few minutes later.

"And if there's one thing worse than sticky food, it's *deep* food. Flat food's not so bad after all."

WILLIAM'S NEW YEAR'S DAY

RICHMAL CROMPTON

WILLIAM WENT WHISTLING DOWN THE STREET, his hands in his pockets. William's whistle was more penetrating than melodious. Sensitive people fled shuddering at the sound. The proprietor of the sweet-shop, however, was not sensitive. He nodded affably as William passed. William was a regular customer of his – as regular, that is, as a wholly inadequate allowance would permit. Encouraged William paused at the doorway and ceased to whistle.

"'Ullo, Mr Moss!" he said.

"'Ullo, William!" said Mr Moss.

"Anythin' cheap today?" went on William hopefully.

Mr Moss shook his head.

"Twopence an ounce cheapest," he said.

William sighed.

"That's awful *dear*," he said.

"What isn't dear? Tell me that. What isn't dear?" said Mr Moss lugubriously.

"Well, gimme two ounces. I'll pay you tomorrow," said William casually.

Mr Moss shook his head.

81

"Go on!" said William. "I get my money tomorrow. You know I get my money tomorrow."

"Cash, young sir," said Mr Moss heavily. "My terms is cash. 'Owever," he relented, "I'll give you a few over when the scales is down tomorrow for a New Year's gift."

"Honest Injun?"

"Honest Injun."

"Well, gimme them now then," said William.

Mr Moss hesitated.

"They wouldn't be no New Year's gift then, would they?" he said.

William considered.

"I'll eat 'em today but I'll *think* about 'em tomorrow," he promised. "That'll make 'em a New Year's gift."

Mr Moss took out a handful of assorted fruit drops and passed them to William. William received them gratefully.

"An' what good resolution are you going to take tomorrow?" went on Mr Moss.

William crunched in silence for a minute, then,

"Good resolution?" he questioned. "I ain't got none."

"You've got to have a good resolution for New Year's Day," said Mr Moss firmly.

"Same as giving up sugar in tea in Lent and wearing blue on Oxford and Cambridge Boat Race Day?" said William with interest.

"Yes, same as that. Well, you've got to think of some fault you'd like to cure and start tomorrow."

William pondered.

"Can't think of anything," he said at last. "You think of something for me."

"You might take one to do your school work properly," he suggested.

William shook his head.

"No," he said, "that wun't be much fun, would it? Crumbs! It *wun't!*"

"Or – to keep your clothes tidy?" went on his friend.

William shuddered at the thought.

"Or to – give up shouting and whistling."

William crammed two more sweets into his mouth and shook his head very firmly.

"Crumbs, no!" he ejaculated indistinctly.

"Or to be perlite."

"Perlite?"

"Yes. 'Please' and 'thank you' and 'if you don't mind me sayin' so' and 'if you excuse me contradictin' of you' and 'can I do anything for you?' and such like."

William was struck with this.

"Yes, I might be that," he said. He straightened his collar and stood up. "Yes, I might try bein' that. How long has it to go on, though?"

"Not long," said Mr Moss. "Only the first day gen'rally. Folks gen'rally give 'em up after that."

"What's yours?" said William, putting four sweets into his mouth as he spoke.

Mr Moss looked round his little shop with the air of a conspirator, then leant forward confidentially.

"I'm goin' to arsk 'er again," he said.

"Who?" said William mystified.

"Someone I've arsked regl'ar every New Year's Day for ten years."

"Asked what?" said William, gazing sadly at his last sweet.

"Arsked to take me, o' course," said Mr Moss with an air of contempt for William's want of intelligence.

"Take you where?" said William. "Where d'you want to go? Why can't you go yourself?"

"Ter *marry* me, I means," said Mr Moss, blushing slightly as he spoke.

"Well," said William with a judicial air, "I wun't have asked the same one for ten years. I'd have tried someone else. I'd have gone on asking other people, if I wanted to get married. You'd be sure to find someone that wouldn't mind you – with a sweet-shop, too. She must be a softie. Does she *know* you've got a sweet-shop?"

Mr Moss merely sighed and popped a Bull's Eye into his mouth with an air of abstracted melancholy.

The next morning William leapt out of bed with an expression of stern resolve. "I'm goin' to be p'lite," he remarked to his bedroom furniture. "I'm goin' to be p'lite all day."

He met his father on the stairs as he went down to breakfast.

"Good mornin', Father," he said, with what he fondly imagined to be a courtly manner. "Can I do anything for you today?"

His father looked down at him suspiciously.

"What do you want now?" he demanded.

William was hurt.

"I'm only bein' p'lite. It's – you know – one of those things you take on New Year's Day. Well, I've took one to be p'lite."

His father apologised. "I'm sorry," he said. "You see, I'm not used to it. It startled me."

At breakfast William's politeness shone forth in all its glory.

"Can I pass you anything, Robert?" he said sweetly.

His elder brother coldly ignored him. "Going to rain again," he said to the world in general.

"If you'll 'scuse me contradicting of you Robert," said William, "I heard the milkman sayin' it was goin' to be fine. If you'll 'scuse me contradictin' you."

"Look here!" said Robert angrily. "Less of your cheek!"

"Seems to me no one in this house understands wot bein' p'lite is," said William bitterly. "Seems to me one might go on bein' p'lite in this house for years an' no one know wot one was doin'."

His mother looked at him anxiously.

"You're feeling quite well, dear, aren't you?" she said. "You haven't got a headache or anything, have you?"

"No. I'm bein' *p'lite*," he said irritably, then pulled himself up suddenly. "I'm quite well, thank you, Mother dear," he said in a tone of cloying sweetness.

"Does it hurt you much?" inquired his brother tenderly.

"No thank you, Robert," said William politely.

After breakfast he received his pocket-money with courteous gratitude.

"Thank you very much, Father."

"Not at all. Pray, don't mention it, William. It's quite all right," said Mr Brown, not to be out-done. Then, "It's rather trying. How long does it last?"

"What?"

"The resolution."

"Oh, bein' p'lite! He said they didn't often do it after the first day."

"He's quite right, whoever he is," said Mr Brown. "They don't."

"He's going to ask her again," volunteered William.

"Who asked who what?" said Mr Brown, but William had departed. He was already on his way to Mr Moss's shop.

Mr Moss was at the door, hatted and coated, and gazing anxiously down the street.

"Goo' mornin' Mr Moss," said William politely.

Mr Moss took out a large antique watch.

"He's late!" he said. "I shall miss the train. Oh, dear! It will be the first New Year's Day I've missed in ten years."

William was inspecting the sweets with the air of an expert.

"Them pink ones are new," he said at last. "How much are they?"

"Eightpence a quarter. Oh, dear, I shall miss the train."

"They're very small ones," said William disparagingly. "You'd think they'd be less than that – small ones like that."

"Will you – will you do something for me and I'll *give* you a quarter of those sweets."

William gasped. The offer was almost too munificent to be true.

"I'll do *anythin'* for that," he said simply.

"Well, just stay in the shop till my nephew Bill comes. 'E'll be 'ere in two shakes an' I'll miss my train if I don't go now. 'E's goin' to keep the shop for me till I'm back an' 'e'll be 'ere any minute now. Jus' tell 'im I 'ad to run for to catch my train an' if anyone comes into the shop before 'e comes jus' tell 'em to wait or to come back later. You can weigh yourself a quarter o' those sweets."

Mr Moss was certainly in a holiday mood. William pinched himself just to make sure that he was still alive and had not been translated suddenly to the realms of the blest.

Mr Moss, with a last anxious glance at his watch, hurried off in the direction of the station.

85

William was left alone. He spent a few moments indulging in roseate day dreams. The ideal of his childhood – perhaps of everyone's childhood – was realized. He had a sweet-shop. He walked round the shop with a conscious swagger, pausing to pop into his mouth a Butter Ball – composed, as the label stated, of pure farm cream and best butter. It was all his – all those rows and rows of gleaming bottles of sweets of every size and colour, those boxes and boxes of attractively arranged chocolates. Deliberately he imagined himself as their owner. By the time he had walked round the shop three times he believed that he was the owner.

At this point a small boy appeared in the doorway. William scowled at him.

"Well," he said ungraciously, "what d'you want!" Then, suddenly remembering his resolution, "*Please* what d'you want?"

"Where's Uncle?" said the small boy with equal ungraciousness. "'Cause our Bill's ill an' can't come."

William waved him off.

"That's all right," he said "You tell 'em that's all right. That's quite all right. See? Now, you go off!"

The small boy stood, as though rooted to the spot. William pressed into one of his hands a stick of liquorice and into the other a packet of chocolate.

"Now, you go *away!* I don't *want* you here. See? You *go away* you little – assified cow!"

William's invective was often wholly original.

The small boy made off, still staring and clutching his spoils. William started to the door and yelled to the retreating figure, "if you don't mind me sayin' so."

He had already come to look upon the Resolution as a kind of god who must at all costs be propitiated. Already the Resolution seemed to have bestowed upon him the dream of his life – a fully-equipped sweet-shop.

He wandered round again and discovered a wholly new sweetmeat called Cokernut Kisses. Its only drawback was its instability. It melted away in the mouth at once. So much so that almost before William was aware of it he was confronted by the empty box. He returned to the more solid charms of the Pineapple Crisp.

He was interrupted by the entrance of a thin lady of uncertain age.

"Good morning," she said icily. "Where's Mr Moss?"

William answered as well as the presence of five sweets in his mouth would allow him.

"I can't hear a word you say," she said – more frigidly than ever.

William removed two of his five sweets and placed them temporarily on the scales.

"Gone," he said laconically, then murmured vaguely, "thank you" as the thought of the Resolution loomed up in his mind.

"Who's in charge?"

"Me," said William ungrammatically.

She looked at him with distinct disapproval.

"Well, I'll have one of those bars of chocolate."

William, looking round the shop, realized suddenly that his own depredations had been on no small scale. But there was a chance of making good any loss that Mr Moss might otherwise have sustained.

He looked down at the twopenny bars.

"Shillin' each," he said firmly.

She gasped.

"They were only twopence yesterday."

"They've gone up since," said William brazenly, adding a vague, "if you'll kin'ly 'scuse me sayin' so."

"Gone up?" she repeated indignantly. "Have you heard from the makers they're gone up?"

"Yes'm," said William politely.

"When did you hear?"

"This mornin' – if you don't mind me sayin' so."

William's manner of fulsome politeness seemed to madden her.

"Did you hear by post?"

"Yes'm. By post this mornin'."

She glared at him with vindictive triumph.

"I happen to live opposite, you wicked, lying boy, and I know that the postman did not call here this morning."

William met her eye calmly.

"No, they came round to see me in the night – the makers did. You cou'n't of heard them," he added hastily. "It was when you was asleep. If you'll 'scuse me contradictin' of you."

It is a great gift to be able to lie so as to convince other people. It is a still greater gift to be able to lie so as to convince oneself. William was possessed of the latter gift.

"I shall certainly not pay any more than twopence," said his customer severely, taking a bar of chocolate and laying down twopence on the counter. "And I shall report this shop to the Profiteering Committee. It's scandalous. And a pack of wicked lies!"

William scowled at her.

"They're a *shillin'*," he said. "I don't want your nasty ole tuppences. I said they was a *shillin'*."

He followed her to the door. She was crossing the street to her house. "You – you ole *thief!*" he yelled after her, though, true to his Resolution, he added softly with dogged determination, "if you don't mind me sayin' so."

"I'll set the police on you," his late customer shouted angrily back across the street. "You wicked, blasphemous boy!"

William put out his tongue at her, then returned to the shop and closed the door.

Here he discovered that the door, when opened, rang a bell, and, after filling his mouth with Liquorice All Sorts, he spent the next five minutes vigorously opening and shutting the door till something went wrong with the mechanism of the bell. At this he fortified himself with a course of Nutty Footballs and, standing on a chair, began ruthlessly to dismember the bell. He was disturbed by the entry of another customer. Swallowing a Nutty Football whole, he hastened to his post behind the counter.

The newcomer was a little girl of about nine – a very dainty little girl, dressed in a white fur coat and cap and long white gaiters. Her hair fell in golden curls over her white fur shoulders.

Her eyes were blue. Her cheeks were velvety and rosy. Her mouth was like a baby's. William had seen this vision on various occasions in the town, had never yet addressed it. Whenever he had seen it, his heart in the midst of his body had been even as melting wax. He smiled – a self-conscious, sheepish smile. His freckled face blushed to the roots of his short stubby hair. She seemed to find nothing odd in the fact of a small boy being in charge of a sweet-shop. She came up to the counter.

"Please, I want two twopenny bars of chocolate."

Her voice was very clear and silvery.

Ecstasy rendered William speechless. His smile grew wider and more foolish. Seeing his two half-sucked Pineapple Crisps exposed upon the scales he hastily put them into his mouth.

She laid four pennies on the counter.

William found his voice.

"You can have lots for that," he said huskily. "They've gone cheap. They've gone ever so cheap. You can take all that boxful for that," he went on recklessly. He pressed the box into her reluctant hands. "An' – what else would you like? You jus' tell me that. Tell me what else you'd like?"

"Please, I haven't any more money," gasped a small, bewildered voice.

"*Money* don't matter," said William. "Things is cheap today. Things is awful cheap today. *Awful* cheap! You can have – anythin' you like for that fourpence. Anythin' you like."

"'Cause it's New Year's Day?" said the vision, with a gleam of understanding.

"Yes," said William, "'cause it's that."

"Is it your shop?"

"Yes," said William with an air of importance. "It's all my shop."

She gazed at him in admiration and envy.

"I'd love to have a sweet-shop," she said wistfully.

"Well, you can take anythin' you like," said William generously.

She collected as much as she could carry and started towards the door. "*Sank* you! Sank you ever so!" she said gratefully.

William stood leaning against the door in the easy attitude of the good-natured, all-providing male.

89

"It's all right," he said with an indulgent smile. "Quite all right. Quite all right." Then with an inspiration born of memories of his father earlier in the day. "Not at all. Don't menshun it. Not at all. Quite all right."

He stopped, simply for lack of further expressions, and bowed with would-be gracefulness as she went through the doorway.

As she passed the window she was rewarded by a spreading effusive smile in a flushed face.

She stopped and kissed her hand.

William blinked with pure emotion.

He continued his smile long after its recipient had disappeared. Then absent-mindedly he crammed his mouth with a handful of Mixed Dew Drops and sat down behind the counter.

As he crunched the Mixed Dew Drops he indulged in a day dream in which he rescued the little girl in the white fur coat from robbers and pirates and a burning house. He was just leaping nimbly from the roof of the burning house, holding the little girl in the white fur coat in his arms, when he caught sight of two of his friends flattening their noses at the window. He rose from his seat and went to the door

"'Ullo Ginger! 'Ullo, Henry!" he said with an unsuccessful effort to appear void of self-consciousness.

They gazed at him in wonder.

"I've gotta shop," he went on casually. "Come on in an' look at it."

They peeped round the door-way cautiously and, reassured by the sight of William obviously in sole possession, they entered, open-mouthed. They gazed at the boxes and bottles of sweets. Aladdin's Cave was nothing to this.

"Howd' you get it, William?" gasped Ginger.

"Someone gave it to me," said William. "I took one of them things to be p'lite an' someone gave it me. Go on," he said kindly. "Jus' help yourselves. Not at all. Jus' help yourselves an' don't menshun it."

They needed no second bidding. With the unerring instinct of childhood (not unsupported by experience) that at any minute their Eden might be invaded by the avenging angel in the shape of a grown-up, they made full use of their time. They went from box to box, putting handfuls of sweets and chocolates into their mouths. They said nothing, simply because speech was, under the circumstances, a physical impossibility. Showing a foresight for the future, worthy of the noble ant itself, so often held up as a model to childhood, they filled pockets in the intervals of cramming their mouths.

A close observer might have noticed that William now ate little. William himself had been conscious for some time of a curious and inexplicable feeling of coldness towards the tempting dainties around him. He was, however, loath to give in to the weakness, and every now and then he nonchalantly put into his mouth a Toasted Square or a Fruity Bit.

It happened that a loutish boy of about fourteen was passing the shop. At the sight of three small boys rapidly consuming the contents, he became interested.

"What yer doin' of?" he said indignantly, standing in the doorway.

"You get out of my shop," said William valiantly.

"*Yer* shop?" said the boy. "Yer bloomin' well pinchin' things out o' someone else's shop, *I* can see. 'Ere, gimme me some of them."

"You get *out*!" said William.

"Get out *yerself*!" said the other.

"If I'd not took one to be p'lite," said William threateningly, "I'd knock you down."

"Yer would, would yer?" said the other, beginning to roll up his sleeves.

"Yes, an' I would, too. You get out." Seizing the nearest bottle, which happened to contain Acid Drops, he began to fire them at his opponent's head. One hit him in the eye. He retired into the street. William, now a-fire for battle, followed him, still hurling Acid Drops with all his might. A crowd of boys collected together. Some gathered Acid Drops from the gutter, others joined the scrimmage. William, Henry, and Ginger carried on a noble fight against heavy odds.

It was only the sight of the proprietor of the shop coming briskly down the side-walk that put an end to the battle. The street boys made off (with what spoils they could gather) in one direction and Ginger and Henry in another. William, clasping an empty Acid Drop bottle to his bosom, was left to face Mr Moss.

Mr Moss entered and looked round with an air of bewilderment.

"Where's Bill?" he said.

"He's ill," said William. "He couldn't come. I've been keepin' shop for you. I've done the best I could." He looked round the riffled shop and hastened to propitiate the owner as far as possible. "I've got some money for you," he added soothingly, pointing to the four pennies that represented his morning's takings. "It's not much," he went on with some truth, looking again at the rows of emptied boxes and half-emptied bottles and the *débris* that is always and everywhere the inevitable result of a battle. But Mr Moss hardly seemed to notice it.

"Thanks, William," he said almost humbly. "William, she's took me. She's goin' ter marry me. Isn't it grand? After all these years!"

"I'm afraid there's a bit of a mess," said William, returning to the more important matter.

Mr Moss waved aside his apologies.

"It doesn't matter, William," he said. "Nothing matters today. She's took me at last. I'm goin' to shut up shop this afternoon and go over to her again. Thanks for staying, William."

"Not at all. Don't menshun it," said William nobly. Then, "I think I've had enough of that bein' p'lite. Will one mornin' do for this year, d'you think?"

"Er – yes. Well, I'll shut up. Don't you stay, William. You'll want to be getting home for lunch."

Lunch? Quite definitely William decided that he did not want any lunch. The very thought of lunch brought with it a feeling of active physical discomfort which was much more than mere absence of hunger. He decided to go home as quickly as possible, though not to lunch.

"Goo' bye," he said.

"Goodbye," said Mr Moss.

"I'm afraid you'll find some things gone," said William faintly; "some boys was in."

"That's all right, William," said Mr Moss, roused again from his rosy dreams. That's quite all right."

But it was not "quite all right" with William. Reader, if you had been left, at the age of eleven, in sole charge of a sweet-shop for a whole morning, would it have been "all right" with you? I trust not. But humiliating hours of the afternoon. We will leave him as, pale and unsteady, but as yet master of the situation, he wends his homeward way.

THE DAY OF JUDGEMENT

RICHARD PECK

In A Long Way from Chicago, *every summer Joey and Mary Alice leave the big city to spend a week with their grandmother in her small country town. The kids are sure that they will be bored, but they are soon proven wrong. Grandma is no ordinary old lady, as this story set in 1932 shows.*

"I DON'T THINK Grandma's a very good influence on us," Mary Alice said. It had taken her a while to come to that conclusion, and I had to agree. It reconciled us some to our trips to visit her. Mary Alice was ten now. I believe this was the first year she didn't bring her jump rope with her. And she no longer pitched a fit because she couldn't take her best friends, Beverly and Audrey, to meet Grandma. "They wouldn't understand," Mary Alice said.

We weren't so sure Mother and Dad would either. Since we still dragged our heels about going, they didn't notice we looked forward to the trip.

The gooseberries were ripe when we got there that August. And come to find out, Grandma was famous for her gooseberry pies. Mary Alice and I were stemming berries at the kitchen table that first morning. Grandma was supervising a pan of them on the stove. The gooseberries popped softly as they burst open in boiling water.

Then somebody knocked on the front door. Grandma ran an arm across her forehead and started through the house. We'd have followed, but she said, "Keep at it."

When she came back, Mrs L. J. Weidenbach, the banker's wife, was right behind her. If she'd thought she was going to be asked to sit down, she had another think coming. Grandma returned to the stove, leaving Mrs Weidenbach beached by the kitchen table, where she overlooked Mary Alice and me.

She was big on top, though nowhere near as big as Grandma. But she had tiny feet, teetering in high-heeled shoes. The heat of the kitchen staggered her, but then people from Death Valley would have keeled over in Grandma's kitchen.

"Mrs Dowdel, I am here on a mission," she said, "and I'll come right to the point."

"Do that," Grandma said.

"As you know, this is county fair week," Mrs Weidenbach said, "the annual opportunity for our small community to make its mark."

Grandma said nothing.

"As you recall," Mrs Weidenbach said, "my bread-and-butter pickles have taken the blue ribbon every year since the fair recommenced after the Great War."

If Grandma recalled this, she showed no sign.

"But my cucumbers this year haven't been up to snuff, not worth the brine for pickling. How were yours?"

"Didn't put any in," Grandma said.

"Ah well, you were wise." Mrs Weidenbach's forehead began to look slick. It wasn't just the heat. "Mrs Dowdel, I'll come clean. I don't think I better enter my bread-and-butter pickles this year, and I'm going to tell you why. The depression is upon us. Times are hard."

"They was never easy for me," Grandma recalled.

"And quite unfairly," Mrs Weidenbach said, "people blame the bankers."

"My stars," Grandma said. "The bank forecloses on people's farms and throws them off their land, and they don't even appreciate it."

"Now, Mrs Dowdel, don't be like that." Mrs Weidenbach reached down the front of her dress and plucked up a lace handkerchief. She dabbed all around her mouth. "Mr Weidenbach has asked me not to enter my bread-and-butter pickles into competition at the fair this year."

"Keep your head down till the depression blows over?"

"Something like that," Mrs Weidenbach murmured. "So I naturally thought of you. After all, we've been neighbours these many years."

The Weidenbachs lived at the far end of town in the only brick house.

"I said to my husband, Mr Weidenbach, somebody must carry home a blue ribbon to keep our town's name in front of the public. Otherwise, those county seat women will sweep the field. As you know, Mrs Cowgill's decorative butter pats never do better than Honourable Mention."

If Grandma knew who won what at the county fair, she showed no sign.

"But there is nobody to touch you for baking with gooseberries. Even those of us who've never had a taste have heard. Word gets around."

"Try as a person will to keep it quiet," Grandma said.

"Gooseberries are tricky things," Mrs Weidenbach went on. "Now, you take Mrs Vottsmeier over at Bement. She wouldn't take on a gooseberry, but she'll pull down a blue ribbon in the Fruit Pies and Cobblers division with her individual cherry tarts if somebody doesn't put a stop to her."

Quiet followed as we listened to Grandma's wooden spoon scraping the sides of the stew pan. At length, she said, "I cook to eat, not to show off."

Mrs Weidenbach sighed. "Mrs Dowdel, these are desperate times. Don't hide your light under a bushel. It is up to you to hold high the banner for our town."

Grandma putting herself out for the fame of the town? I thought Mrs Weidenbach was on the wrong track. On the other hand, Grandma liked to win.

Growing frantic, Mrs Weidenbach let her gaze skim over Mary

Alice and me. "And a day at the fair would be a nice outing for your grandkiddies."

"Wouldn't cut any ice with them," Grandma said. "They're from Chicago, so they've seen everything."

Instantly, an expression of great boredom fell over Mary Alice's face. I thought she might yawn. She was playing along with Grandma. I'd been thinking a day at the fair would be a welcome change, but I just shrugged and went on stemming gooseberries.

Grandma turned slightly from the stove. "Wouldn't have any way to get there if I wanted to go."

Mrs Weidenbach brightened. "I will personally conduct you to the fair on prize day in my Hupmobile." She waved a hand in benediction over us. "And there'll be plenty of room for your grandkiddies."

"Oh well," Grandma said, "if I have an extra pie and it's not raining that day . . ."

"Mrs Dowdel, I knew you would stand and deliver!" Mrs Weidenbach clasped her hands. "And remember, even the red ribbon for second prize will be better than nothing."

Grandma gazed past her, seeming to count the corpses on the flypaper strip. Mrs Weidenbach was dismissed and soon left. We all listened to the powerful roar as she ground her Hupmobile into gear.

Grandma's sleeves were already turned back, or she'd be turning them back now. She pointed at me. "Scoot uptown and bring me a twenty-five-pound sack of sugar. Tell them to stick it on my bill. After that I want every gooseberry off them bushes out back." She turned on Mary Alice. "And you're going to learn a thing or two about pie crust."

There followed three of the busiest days of my young life. Wrestling twenty-five pounds of sugar back from Moore's Store was nothing to picking all the gooseberry bushes clean. As Mrs Weidenbach said, gooseberries are tricky things – sour to the taste and spikey with stickers. Not unlike Grandma. My throbbing hands were covered with sticker wounds from getting all the gooseberries into the pail. With towels around their middles and their hair tucked up, Grandma and Mary Alice rolled out endless pastry on big breadboards.

We baked a gooseberry pie every four hours for the next three days. I had about all I could do to feed corncobs into the stove to keep the oven heat even. Gooseberries are so tart that more sugar than fruit goes into the pie. Some pies were still too sour, others gritty with too much sugar.

We tried and tried again. Grandma grew careful about balancing her ingredients, holding the measuring cup up to the light. She was like a scientist seeking the cure for something. I had to go back uptown for more sugar and another big can of Crisco. And we had to sample them all in search for the perfect pie. Mary Alice says she's never since been able to look a gooseberry in the face.

The day of judgement came. Mary Alice and I were in the parlour early, waiting. Grandma had told us to cover our heads against the fairground sun. I had on the Cubs cap I travelled in, and Mary Alice wore her straw from Easter. The house reeked of baking.

Then Grandma sailed like a galleon into the front room, striking us dumb. For her, dressing up usually meant taking off her apron. But this morning she wore a ready-made dress covered with flowers. The collar was fine net, fixed with a big cameo brooch that rode high. On her feet were large, unfamiliar shoes – white with the hint of a heel, and laces tied in big, perky bows. On her head was a hat with a big brim. The hatband on it happened to be a blue ribbon.

She glared, daring us to pay her a compliment. But the cat had our tongues. Mary Alice stared up at her, transfixed. Was she seeing herself fifty years hence?

The Hupmobile growled up outside, and the next thing you knew, we were in it. It wasn't as long as Al Capone's big Lincoln limousine, but it was the biggest car in this town. Mary Alice and I had the backseat to ourselves. The pie was in a box between my feet.

Grandma took charge of a small hamper full of our lunch,

since they charge you two prices for everything at a fair. She rode up front beside Mrs Weidenbach, with one big elbow propped outside the open window. The town had emptied out because this was prize day at the fair. But when we went by The Coffee Pot Cafe, there were faces at the window, and a loafer or two paused on the sidewalk to see us pass. Grandma inclined her head slightly. Most people wouldn't take their bows till after they'd won a blue ribbon, but Grandma wasn't most people.

The fairground was a pasture along a dusty road this side of the county seat. It was a collection of sheds and tents and a grandstand for the harness racing. But this was the big day for judging cattle, quilts and cookery, so the grounds were packed, though it was a nickel to get in.

Mrs Weidenbach twinkled along in her high heels next to Grandma. She didn't dare show her pickles, but she wanted some reflected glory in case the gooseberry pie won. "Let's run that pie over to the Domestic Sciences tent and get it registered," she said.

"I don't want it setting around," Grandma said. "The livestock draws flies." The pie was no burden to Grandma because I was carrying it. "Let's see something of the fair first," she said, managing to sound uninterested.

Along the midway the Anti-Horse-Thief Society had a stand selling burgoo and roasting ears. The 4-H club was offering chances on a heifer. Allis-Chalmers had a big tent showing their huskers and combines. Prohibition was about to be repealed, but the Temperance people had another big tent, offering ice water inside and a stage out front with a quartet performing. We stopped to hear them:

> You may drive your horse fast if you please,
> You may live in the very best style;
> Smoke the choicest cigars, at your ease,
> And may revel in pleasure awhile;
> Play billiards, from morning till night,
> Or loaf in the barroom all day,

But just see if my words are not right:
You will find, in the end, it don't pay.

At the other end of the midway was a rickety Ferris wheel, a merry-go-round and a caterpillar. Beyond it was a sight that drew me. In an open stubblefield a biplane stood. Beside it was the pilot in a leather helmet with goggles, and puttees wrapped around his legs.

And a sign:

BARNSTORMING BARNIE BUCHANAN
AIR ACE
TRICK FLYING AND PASSENGER RIDES

My heart skipped a beat, and sank. Another sign read:

RIDES 75¢

I didn't have that kind of money on me. I didn't have any money on me. Still, my heart began to taxi. I'd never been in a plane, and my hero was Colonel Charles A. Lindbergh, who'd flown the Atlantic alone.

The American Legion was sponsoring Barnie Buchanan. A red-faced man in a Legionnaire's cap bawled through a megaphone, "Tell you what I'm going to do, folks. Any minute now Mr Buchanan is going to show us his stuff by putting his machine through the same manoeuvers he used in the Great War against the wily Hun. Then if you think six bits is still too steep, Mr Buchanan has agreed to a special prize-day offer. To every blue ribbon winner, Mr Buchanan will give a ride in his plane gratis. That's free of charge, ladies and gentlemen."

My heart left the ground, skimmed a hedgerow, and sailed into the wild blue yonder. The pie in my hands would win first prize since nobody but Grandma would take a chance with gooseberries. But she'd let me have her plane ride because she was too old and too big.

"You reckon that thing will get off the ground?" she said doubtfully, building my hopes higher.

"It looks like a box kite," Mary Alice said. "A person would have to be nuts to go up in it."

The biplane's wings were canvas-covered and much patched. It was more rickety than the Ferris wheel. Still, it was a plane, and this looked like my one chance in life to go up in one. Now Mrs Weidenbach was plucking at Grandma's arm, and it was time to enter the pie into competition.

When we four went into the Domestic Sciences tent, Grandma remarked, "I said there'd be flies." Surrounded by crowds, the long tables were all laid out: jams and preserves, vegetables in novelty shapes, cakes and breads. A half-sized cow carved out of butter reclined on a block of melting ice. It was as hot as Grandma's kitchen in the tent, so people fanned paper fans, compliments of Broshear's Funeral Home, each with the Broshear motto printed on it:

WHEN YOU COME TO THE END,
YOU'LL FIND A FRIEND

Mrs Weidenbach averted her eyes as we passed Pickled Products. I took charge of unpacking the pie and getting it registered at Fruit Pies and Cobblers. Grandma started at the other end of the table, casting an eye over the competition. Everything looked good to me, and I was wishing I was a judge so I could have a taste. A little card with a number and a name stood beside each entry.

When she got to her own pie, Grandma froze. Next to it was another lattice-topped gooseberry pie. There was no doubt about it. Only gooseberries are that shade of grey-green. And it was a very nice-looking pie. The edges of its pastry were as neatly crimped as Grandma's. Maybe better. She bent to read the card, and whipped around.

I followed her look as it fell on one of the smallest people in the tent. It was a man, one of the few there. A little tiny man. He wore small bib overalls, a dress shirt, and a bow tie. Four of five strands of hair were arranged across his little bald head.

"Rupert Pennypacker," Grandma breathed. You seldom saw her caught off guard. Was he responsible for the other gooseberry pie?

"Who?" I said.

"The best home-baker in the state of Illinois," Grandma said. "Him and me come up together out in the country, so I know."

Mrs Weidenbach quaked. Even Mary Alice looked concerned.

"I'm a goner," said Grandma.

A puttering sound deafened us. It was Barnie Buchanan, the air ace, right over our heads. He was doing his aerial stunts: barrel rolls and vertical figure eights, or whatever he did. Everybody looked up, though we could only see tent.

It was just a moment, but somehow I was sure. In that split second when we'd all looked up, I thought Grandma had switched her pie's card with Rupert Pennypacker's. It was a desperate act, but as Mrs Weidenbach had said, these were desperate times. It was the wrong thing for Grandma to do, but I might get a plane ride out of it. My head swam.

Grandma nudged me away from the table and elbowed through a parting crowd. She was making for Mr Pennypacker. I wondered if she'd reach down, grab him by his bib, and fling him out of the tent. With Grandma, you never knew. "Rupert," she said.

Standing beside him was the scariest-looking old lady I'd ever seen, weirder than Aunt Puss Chapman. She was only a little taller than Mr Pennypacker and dressed all in black, including the veil on her hat. She had warts, and her chin met her hat brim. There was a lump in her cheek that looked like it might be a bunch of chaw.

"You remember Mama," Mr Pennypacker said to Grandma.

His voice was high, like it had never changed. My voice hadn't changed either, but I was twelve, so I still had hope.

His old mama hissed something in his ear and tried to pull him away with a claw on his arm.

"Well, may the best man win," Grandma said, turning on her heel. By now the judges were at work. They carried little silver knives and miniature trowels for sampling the cobblers and pies. Tension mounted.

Nervously, Mrs Weidenbach said to Grandma, "What a nice, moist consistency your pie filling has, Mrs Dowdel. I'm sure it will be noted. How much water did you add to the mixture?"

"About a mouthful," Grandma replied.

The judging went on forever, but nobody left the sweltering tent. We all watched the judges chewing. Finally, Mary Alice said she thought she might faint, so I took her outside.

Up among the clouds Barnie Buchanan was still putting his old biplane through its paces. He dived to earth, then pulled up in time. He gave us three loops and a snap roll. And my heart was up there with him, scouting for Germans.

A voice rose from inside the tent, followed by gusts of applause. They were announcing the winners: honourable mention, third prize, second – first. I didn't want to go back in there, I hoped we'd win, but I wasn't sure we should. Not if Grandma had switched –

The tent quivered with one final burst of applause. People began streaming out, flowing around us. Then out strolled Mr Pennypacker and his mama, clutching him. You couldn't read anything in that face of hers, but Mr Pennypacker was beaming. From the clasp on his overall bib hung a blue ribbon.

"Shoot," Mary Alice said. "After all that pie crust I rolled out." In a way I was relieved. But then I saw my one and only chance for a plane ride crash and burn. Mr Pennypacker was already heading for the field where the biplane was coming in for a landing.

At last Mrs Weidenbach and Grandma came out. A nod from Grandma sent me back to the Hupmobile for our hamper of lunch. We ate it at a table in the Temperance tent, sliced chicken washed down with ice water. Grandma had her great stone face on, but Mrs Weidenbach tried to make the best of things.

"Never mind, Mrs Dowdel. As I have said, a red ribbon for second place is not to be sneezed at or scorned. You did right well."

But Grandma didn't come to the fair for second prize. She

didn't wear it, if she'd bothered to collect it at all. "And you were up against stiff competition," Mrs Weidenbach said. "I daresay Rupert Pennypacker has had nothing to do all his life but wait on his dreadful mother and bake."

Consoling Grandma was a thankless task. She ate her chicken sandwich with her usual appetite, observing the crowds. If I could read her mind at all, she was thinking she could do with a cold beer.

The day seemed to have peaked and was going downhill now. As we left the Temperance tent, the quartet was singing, in close harmony:

> *. . . Lips that touch wine*
> *Will never touch mine . . .*

We were ready to head for the parking pasture, but Grandma turned us the other way, towards the midway and the biplane.

"Wha –" said Mrs Weidenbach, but fell silent.

We were walking through the fair, and something inside my rib cage began to stir. There ahead, the biplane was on the ground. Afternoon sun played off the dull mahogany of its propeller. Something within me dared to dream. I wasn't swooping. I didn't even taxi, but I was walking lighter.

Giving blue ribbon winners free rides hadn't stimulated much business. Barnie Buchanan was lounging beside his plane. He was smoking another cigarette in a cupped hand, pilot-style.

Grandma strode past the ticket table, out onto the field. She paused to look the plane over from prop to tail. Then she glanced briefly down at me. I didn't dare look up at her. But my hopes were rising. Then she marched forward. When Barnie Buchanan saw Grandma bearing down on him, he tossed away his cigarette.

"I'm a blue ribbon winner," Grandma announced, "here for my ride."

"Wha –" Mrs Weidenbach said.

My brain went dead.

"Well, ma'am," Barnie Buchanan said uncertainly, noticing her size. "And what class did you compete in?"

"Fruit Pies and Cobblers." She held up a crumpled blue ribbon clutched in her fist. She gave him a glimpse of it, then dropped the ribbon into her pocketbook.

"Well, ma'am, it seems to me I've already given a ride to a man who won first in pies," he said. "A little fellow."

"Oh that's Rupert Pennypacker," Grandma said. "You got that turned around in your mind. He won in Sausage and Headcheese. Don't I look more like a pie baker than him?"

Grandma reached up to pull the pin out of her hat. She handed the hat to Mary Alice. "Here, hold this. It might blow off." I saw the hatband was missing from her hat, the blue ribbon.

It took three members of the American Legion and Barnie Buchanan to get Grandma into the front cockpit of the plane. Eventually, the sight drew a crowd. The Legionnaires would invite Grandma to step into their clasped hands, then boost her up. That didn't work.

Then they'd hoist her up some other way, but she'd get halfway there, and her hindquarters would be higher than her head. They had an awful job getting her into the plane, and they were wringing wet. But at last she slid into the seat, to a round of applause from the crowd. Grandma was a tight fit, and the plane seemed to bend beneath her. Barnie Buchanan stroked his chin. But then he pulled his goggles over his eyes and sprang up to the rear seat. He could pilot the plane from there, if he could see around Grandma. A Legionnaire jerked the propeller and the motor coughed twice then roared.

Mrs Weidenbach was between Mary Alice and me now, clutching our hands.

A lot of Grandma stuck up above the plane. The breeze stirred her white hair, loosening the bun on the back. Her spectacle lenses flashed like goggles. She raised one hand in farewell, and the plane began to bump down the field.

Now my heart was in my mouth. Everyone's was. The biplane, heavy-burdened, lumbered over uneven ground,

trying to gather speed. It drew nearer and nearer the hedgerow at the far end of the field.

"Lift!" the crowd cried. "Lift!" Mary Alice's hands were over her eyes.

But then distant dust spurted from the plane's front wheels. The tail rose, but dropped down again. It had stopped just short of the hedgerow, and now it was turning back. We watched the bright disc of the whirling propeller as the biplane returned to us.

Barnie Buchanan dropped down from the cockpit. He looked pale, shaken. Boy, did he need a cigarette. But they had to get Grandma down from the plane, and getting her out was twice the job of getting her in. She'd plant one big shoe on a shoulder and the other on another. They had her by the ankles, then by the hips. She tipped forward and back, and the pocketbook swinging from her arm pummelled their heads. She brought two big men to their knees.

At last she was on solid ground, scanning the crowd for me. She crooked a finger, and I went forth. As always, I couldn't see a moment ahead.

"Ma'am, I'm sorry," Barnie Buchanan was saying to Grandma. "But I was just carrying a little more . . . freight than this old crate could handle."

Grandma waved that away. "Don't give it a thought. You can take my grandson instead," she said. "If he wants to go."

The heavens opened. I thought I heard celestial music. Somehow I was up in the front seat of the plane, buckling myself in with trembling hands. And Barnie Buchanan was handing me up a pair of goggles. Goggles from the Great War.

Now we were taxiing, Barnie and me, bumping over the ground, gathering speed behind the yearning motor. And I felt that moment when we left the ground, and the fair fell away below us, and ahead of us was nothing but the towering white clouds. And beyond them sky, endless sky. I didn't know there was that much sky, as we flew, Barnie and me, in stuttering circles higher than birds, over the patchwork fields.

That night Mary Alice went up to bed early, tuckered out. Still in her fair finery, Grandma sat in the platform rocker, working out of her shoes. They'd been a torment to her all day. Now she kicked them aside. "If I could pop all the corns on my toes," she said, "I could feed a famine."

I'd settled on the settee, watching her in the circle of light, after the big doings of the day.

"Grandma," I said at last. "I've got a couple of things on my mind."

"Well, spit 'em out," she said, "if you must."

"About your plane ride. You never did expect it to get off the ground, did you?"

"Lands no." She turned down a hand. "When I was dainty enough for a plane to lift, they didn't have them. We couldn't have dusted the crops with me on board. I just wanted to see what it felt like sitting up there in that hen roost."

"Cockpit, Grandma," I said. "Then you meant for me to have the ride all along?"

Grandma didn't reply.

"And another thing. I've got a confession to make," I said. "I know you wanted first prize on the pie. You wanted it bad. And I thought you'd switched the card on Mr Pennypacker's pie with yours so you could win with his pie."

She shot me her sternest look. But then easing back in the platform rocker, she said, "I did."

THE YELLOW RIBBON

MARIA LEACH
Adapted by VIRGINIA TASHJIAN

ONCE THERE WAS A BOY NAMED JOHN and a girl named Jane. John loved Jane very much. They lived next door to each other, and they went to nursery school together.

Every day John would carry Jane's books to school and every day Jane wore a yellow ribbon around her neck.

One day John said, "Jane, why do you wear that yellow ribbon around your neck?"

"I can't tell," said Jane, "and anyway I don't feel like telling you." But John kept on asking, and finally Jane said perhaps she'd tell him later sometime.

The next year John and Jane were in the infant school. One day John asked again, "Janey, why do you wear that yellow ribbon around your neck?"

"It's not really your affair, John; perhaps I'll tell you sometime . . . but not now," said Jane.

Time went by; John still loved Jane and Jane loved John. And John carried Jane's books to school and Jane wore the yellow ribbon around her neck. They were in the junior school . . . then secondary school. And every once in a while John asked Jane why she wore the yellow ribbon, but Jane never told. "We've been friends a long time, John, what difference does it make?" she said. And so time went by.

John and Jane went through secondary school together. John still loved Jane and Jane loved John. John carried Jane's books to school and Jane still wore the yellow ribbon around her neck. On the last day John said, "Jane, we're leaving school now. Won't you *please* tell me why you wear that yellow ribbon around your neck?"

"Oh, John," said Jane, "there's no point in telling you now . . . but some day I will." And that day passed.

Time went by, and John still loved Jane and Jane loved John and Jane still wore that yellow ribbon around her neck.

One day, John and Jane became engaged.

"Why do you wear that yellow ribbon around your neck, Jane love?" said John, and finally Jane said perhaps she would tell him why on their wedding day.

But the wedding day came, and what with all the preparations for the wedding and the honeymoon, John just forgot to ask. But several days later, John asked Jane why she wore that yellow ribbon around her neck.

"Well, we are happily married and we love each other, so what difference does it make, John?" said Jane. So John let that pass, but he still *did* want to know.

Time went by. John loved Jane and Jane loved John. Lovely children were born to them, and they were so busy bringing them up that before they knew it, it was their golden wedding anniversary.

"Jane, why do you wear that yellow ribbon around your neck?" asked John once more. And Jane said, "Since you have waited this long, you can wait a little longer. I'll tell you some day, John."

Time went by. John loved Jane and Jane loved John. Finally, Jane was taken very ill and was dying. John bent on his knees by her bedside, and with sobs in his voice asked, "Janey, *please* tell me: Why do you wear that yellow ribbon around your neck?"

"All right, John. You may untie it now," said Jane.

So John did . . . AND JANE'S HEAD FELL OFF!

THE SHIP OF FOOLS

TERRY JONES

A YOUNG BOY NAMED BEN once ran away to sea. But the ship he joined was a very odd one indeed.

The Captain always wore his trousers tied over his head with seaweed. The Bosun danced the hornpipe all day long from dawn to dusk wearing nothing but beetroot juice. And the First Mate kept six families of mice down the neck of his jumper!

"This is a rum vessel, me hearty!" said Ben to one of the sailors, who was at that moment about to put his head into the ship's barrel of syrup.

"It's a Ship of Fools!" grinned the sailor, and he stuck his head in the syrup.

"I suppose you all must know what you're doing," murmured young Ben, but the sailor couldn't reply because he was all stuck up with syrup.

Just then the Captain yelled: "Raise the hanky! And sit on the snails!" Although, because he still had his trousers over his head, what it actually sounded like was "Gmpf der wmfky! Umf bmfwmf umf wmf!"

"I'm sure he means: 'Raise the anchor! And set the sails!'" said young Ben to himself. But whatever it was the Captain had said, nobody seemed to be taking the slightest bit of notice.

"They must be doing more important things," said Ben to himself. "So I suppose *I'd* better obey Captain's orders."

So Ben raised the anchor by himself, and hoisted the sails as best he could, and the ship sailed off into the blue.

"Where are we heading, shipmate?" Ben asked a sailor who was hanging over the side, trying to paint the ship with a turnip and a pot of lemonade.

"Goodness knows!" exclaimed the sailor. "It's a Ship of Fools!"

"The Captain will know," said Ben, and he climbed up to the bridge, where the Captain was standing upside-down at the wheel, trying to steer with his feet.

"I'm almost sure you shouldn't steer a ship like that," said Ben to himself, "but then what do I know? I'm just a raw land-lubber getting his first taste of the briney." But even so, Ben realized that the Captain couldn't see where they were going, because his trousers were still over his eyes. As it happened, the ship was, at that moment, heading straight for a lighthouse! So Ben grabbed the wheel, and said: "What's the course, skipper?"

"Bmf Bmf Wmf!" replied the Captain.

"Nor' Nor' West it is, sir!" said Ben, and he steered the ship safely round the lighthouse and off for the open sea.

Well, they hadn't sailed very far before a storm blew up.

"Shall I take in the yard-arm and reef the sails, Captain?" yelled Ben. But the Captain was far too busy trying to keep his game of marbles still, as the ship rolled from side to side.

The wind began to howl, and the sea grew angry.

"I better had, anyway," said Ben to himself, and he ran about the ship, preparing for the storm ahead.

As he did so, the rest of the crew grinned and waved at him, but they all carried on doing whatever it was they were doing. One of them was hanging by his hair from the mainmast, trying to play the violin with a spoon. Another was varnishing his nose with the ship's varnish. While another was trying to stretch his ears by tying them to the capstan and jumping overboard.

"Well ... I wouldn't have thought this was the way to run a ship!" said young Ben. "I suppose they know the ropes and I'm just learning. Even so . . . I didn't realize the newest recruit had to do *everything*! But I suppose I'd better get on with it." And he set about doing what he thought should be done, while the rest of the crew just grinned and waved at him.

The storm gathered force, and soon great waves were lashing across the deck as the ship rolled and wallowed. Ben rushed about trying to get everyone below decks, so he could batten down the hatches. But as soon as he got one sailor to go below, another would pop up from somewhere else.

And all the time, the ship rolled, and before long it began to take on water.

"Cap'n! We must get the men below decks and batten down the hatches, while we ride out the storm!" yelled Ben.

But the Captain had decided to take his supper on the fo'c'sle, and was far too busy – trying to keep the waves off his lamb chop with an egg whisk – to listen to Ben.

And still the ship took on more water.

"She's beginning to list!" shouted Ben. "The hold's filling with water!"

"It's OK!" said the Bosun, who had stopped doing the hornpipe, but was still only wearing beetroot juice. "Look!" and he held up a large piece of wood.

"What's that?" gasped Ben.

"It's the ship's bung!" said the Bosun proudly. "Now any water will run out through the bunghole in the bottom of the ship!"

"You're a fool!" yelled Ben.

"I know!" grinned the Bosun. "It's a Ship of Fools!"

"Now we'll sink for sure!" cried Ben.

And, sure enough, the ship began to sink.

"Man the lifeboats!" yelled Ben. But the fools had all climbed up the mast and were now clinging to it, playing conkers and "I Spy With My Little Eye".

So Ben had to launch the lifeboat on his own. And he only managed to do it just as the ship finally went down. Then he had to paddle around in the terrible seas, fishing the crew of fools out of the heaving waters.

"I spy with my little eye something beginning with . . . S!"

114

shouted the First Mate, as Ben hauled him into the lifeboat.

"Sea," said Ben wearily, and rowed over to the next fool.

By the time night fell, Ben had managed to get the Captain and the Bosun and the First Mate and all the rest of the crew of fools into the little lifeboat. But they wouldn't keep still, and they kept shouting and laughing and falling overboard again, and Ben had his work cut out trying to keep them all together.

By dawn the storm had died down, and Ben was exhausted, but he'd managed to save everyone. One of the fools, however, had thrown all the oars overboard while Ben hadn't been watching, so they couldn't row anywhere. And now the First Mate was so hungry he'd started to eat the lifeboat!

"You can't eat wood!" yelled Ben.

"You can – if you're fool enough!" grinned the First Mate.

"But if you eat the lifeboat, we'll all drown!" gasped Ben.

"It's a pity we don't have a little pepper and salt," remarked the Captain, who had also started to nibble the boat.

"It's salty enough as it is!" said the Bosun, who was tucking into the rudder.

"Urgh!" said the Chief Petty Officer. "It's uncooked!" You shouldn't eat uncooked lifeboat!"

But they did.

By midday, they'd managed to eat most of the lifeboat, and Ben had just given them all up for lost, when, to his relief, he saw land on the horizon.

"Land ahead!" shouted Ben, and he tried to get the fools to paddle with their hands towards it, but they were feeling a bit sick from all the wood they'd just eaten. So Ben broke off the last plank and used that to paddle them towards the shore.

At last they landed, and the fools all jumped ashore and started filling their trousers with sand and banging their heads on the rocks. While young Ben looked for food.

He hadn't looked very far, when a man with a spear suddenly barred his way.

Ben tried to signal that he meant no harm, that he had been

115

shipwrecked, and that he and his crew-mates were in sore distress. Once the man understood all this, he became very friendly, and offered Ben food and drink. But as soon as the two of them returned to Ben's shipmates, the crew of fools all leaped up making terrible faces and tried to chase the stranger off.

"Stop it!" cried Ben. "He's trying to help us!" But the crew of fools had already jumped on the poor fellow, and started beating and punching him, until eventually he fled back to his village to fetch a war party.

"Now we can't even stay here!" screamed Ben. "You're all fools!"

"Of course we are!" cried the Captain. "We keep telling you – it's a Ship of Fools!"

Now I don't know how what happened next came about, or what would have happened to Ben if it hadn't, but it did. And this is what it was.

Young Ben was just wondering what on earth he was going to do, when a sail appeared on the horizon!

But before Ben could shout out: "There's a ship!", he turned and saw the war party approaching with spears and bows and arrows, while the crew of fools were busy trying to bury the Bosun head-first in the sand.

Ben finally shook his head and said: "Well you've all certainly taught me one thing: and that's not to waste time with those I can see are fools – no matter who they are – Captain, Bosun or First Mate!"

And with that, Ben dived into the sea and swam off to join the other boat. And he left the Ship of Fools to their own fate.

SPELLSHOCKED

FINBAR O'CONNOR

T HE QUEEN WAS HAVING A BABY and outside the royal bedroom the Royal Librarian, the Court Astrologer and the editor of the *Daily Dragon* were waiting eagerly for news.Suddenly the bedroom door flew open and the King rushed out in his nightshirt with his crown perched crookedly on his head.

"It's a boy!" he cried joyfully, doing somersaults around the hallway.

"An heir to the throne!" said the Royal Librarian happily.

"Just as I predicted!" said the Court Astrologer smugly.

"THE BOY WHO WILL BE KING!" scribbled the editor of the *Daily Dragon*. "Our readers will love this!"

"I mean to say," cried the King, dancing on the furniture, "it's a *girl!*"

"An heir*ess* to the throne!" said the Royal Librarian hastily.

"It was all in the stars," said the Court Astrologer complacently.

"THE QUEEN OF OUR HEARTS!" scribbled the editor of the *Daily Dragon*. "Our readers will love this!"

"That is, it's neither, or rather it's both!" cried the King, turning cartwheels down the stairs.

"Are you feeling quite all right, sire?" asked the Royal Librarian anxiously.

"I saw this coming, of course," said the Court Astrologer knowingly.

"KING GOES BONKERS!" scribbled the editor of the *Daily Dragon*. "Our readers will *really* love this!"

"It's twins, you idiots," said the King, flopping down on a sofa and mopping his brow. "A boy *and* a girl."

"Congratulations, sire!" said the Royal Librarian.

"I *said* it would be one or the other," said the Court Astrologer. "I'm never wrong, you know."

"ROYAL MIXED DOUBLES!" scribbled the editor of the *Daily Dragon*. "Oh well, I suppose it'll have to do!"

The King and Queen were delighted with their new babies. Every morning, while the Queen was doing her post-natal exercises, the King rushed down to the nursery to change their nappies before breakfast while the Royal Nanny (who had looked after the King when *he* was a baby) stood by, wringing her hands anxiously and saying, "*Please* be careful, sire!"

"Oh, stop fussing, woman," said the King, as he balanced a baby on each knee and busily powdered their bottoms. "I *am* their father, after all!"

"Your royal father never powdered *your* bottom, Your Majesty," said Nanny crossly. "That was always *my* job!"

"Leave my bottom out of this, Nanny," snapped the King. "And stop being so old-fashioned. This *is* the Middle Ages, you know!"

One morning when the twins were six weeks old and the King was in the nursery as usual, the Queen came in, looking worried.

"Oh, Kingy-Poo?" said the Queen.

"Yes, Queeny-Pie?" replied the King, not taking his eyes off the twins, who were lying in their cot, kicking their legs and gurgling.

"I'm afraid there's trouble in the Kingdom, darling," said the Queen.

"That's nice, precious," replied the King. "Say *Da-Da*, baby. *Da-Da*?"

"A mean old dragon has been devouring people in the Eastern Forest," said the Queen.

"Splendid, splendid!" said the King. "Say *Ma-Ma*, baby. *Ma-Ma*?"

"And a great big giant has been squashing people in the Western Wood," said the Queen.

"Marvellous, wonderful!" said the King. "Which of 'em looks more like me, d'you think?"

The Queen was puzzled for a moment, but then she realized he was talking about the babies.

"Anyway," said the Queen, "I thought I'd just ride out with the knights and slay something, don't you know?"

"Excellent idea, dearest," said the King, who hadn't heard a word. "Have a lovely time!"

So the Queen (who, of course, loved her babies but got bored hanging around the castle all day) galloped off to take care of things in the Kingdom while the King (who, of course, loved his subjects but got bored galloping around slaying things all day) stayed at home and took care of things in the nursery.

Everything went on happily until the twins were a year old and the arrangements for their first birthday got under way. The King was in a good mood because the Court Astrologer had confidently predicted that the weather would be fine (as long as it didn't rain), and the Queen was in a good mood because she loved organizing things.

"I'm sure our readers would like to know who will be at the party," said the editor of the *Daily Dragon* (who was hoping for an invitation).

"Oh, just family," said the King. "Relations, close friends, that sort of thing."

"Say about five hundred in all," added the Queen.

"And birthday cake for all our subjects, of course," chortled the King.

"LET THEM EAT CAKE SAYS KING!" scribbled the editor. "Very generous of you, sire!"

Just then, the Royal Librarian came in.

"Sire," he said, "I have been reading books in the Royal Library."

"Well, that's nothing to be ashamed of, man," said the King jovially. "I read a book myself once!"

"But sire," said the Royal Librarian, "according to these books it is absolutely imperative that you invite a witch to Their Highnesses' birthday party!"

"Invite a witch to my children's party?" spluttered the King. "Have you taken leave of your senses, Librarian?"

"But all the best authorities recommend it, Your Majesty," said the Royal Librarian.

"What authorities are these?" asked the King.

"Well, sire," stammered the Royal Librarian, "there's *My First Book of Fairy Tales* and *Nursery Tales for Tiny Tots* and –"

"Now listen here, Librarian," interrupted the King. "As I keep telling Nanny, this isn't Once-Upon-A-Time any more. We're a modern, progressive kingdom, we are! Why, only last Wednesday we discovered the . . . What do you call that thing that goes round and round? They put 'em on carts and such."

"The wheel, sire?" said the Royal Librarian.

"The wheel, exactly," said the King. "Marvellous invention. Saves a lot of wear and tear on peasants . . . anyway, the point is it's time to forget these old superstitions. So, no witches at my children's party, and no giants, wizards or dragons either, eh what?"

"If you say so, sire," said the Royal Librarian.

"I do say so, sire!" said the King firmly. "You read too many books, Librarian, and that's your trouble! Just forget about books and get on with running the library!"

"Yes, sire," said the Royal Librarian with a sigh.

The day of the party dawned bright and sunny. ("I told you so!" said the Royal Astrologer.) Two long tables were set out in the castle gardens with the King at the head of one and the Queen at the head of the other. The twins sat in high-chairs under the blossoming trees and gurgled and cooed and were admired by everybody. The guests ate and drank and sang and laughed, while the editor of the *Daily Dragon* prowled around eavesdropping on conversations and making notes for his gossip column. The only person who looked unhappy was the Royal Librarian. Suddenly dark clouds blotted out the sun, lightning flashed and there was an ominous roll of thunder. ("Just as I foretold!" said the Royal Astrologer.)

Then a great black raven came flapping across the garden and perched on a branch above the babies' heads. The blossoms withered and fell from the tree as the raven spread its shadowy wings and opened its sword-sharp bill and croaked in a harsh voice:

"SLEEP LIKE DEATH THE OLD KINGS DAUGHTER
OLD KING'S SON SHALL DWELL IN WATER
FOREVER THIS SPELL LASTS UNLESS –"

But even as the raven spoke the King sprang from his seat, snatched a bow from one of the guards, took careful aim and shot an arrow at the bird's black breast.

"No, sire!" cried the Royal Librarian. But he was too late. The raven screeched as the arrow pierced its heart, and fell dead on the ground, scorching the grass where it lay.

("CRACK SHOT KING GETS A BIRDIE!" scribbled the editor of the *Daily Dragon*.)

Black vapour engulfed the raven's body and when it had cleared the bird had vanished and an old witch with a sword-sharp face and a cloak of black feathers lay dead on the ground.

("CALLOUS KING SHOOTS PENSIONER!" scribbled the editor of the *Daily Dragon*.)

"My babies!" cried the Queen in horror, for the Princess lay pale in a sleep like death and where the young Prince had been sitting a hideous green frog squatted and croaked.

"I *knew* this would happen!" sighed the Royal Librarian.

"That's just what *I* was going to say!" said the Court Astrologer.

The King and Queen sat in the throne room and wept.

"I tried to warn you, sire," said the Royal Librarian. "Witches get terribly offended if you don't invite them to birthday parties. They can be very spiteful about things like that."

"I should have listened to you from the start, Librarian," said the King. "You're the only one around here who talks any sense!" (The Court Astrologer looked insulted but said nothing.)

"Sire," said the Librarian, "you did right to kill the witch. But she died before she had finished her spell. If you had waited until the spell was finished it would have told us how to break the enchantment."

"Then what can we do?" asked the King. "Are my children to remain cursed forever?"

"I must study the books in the Royal Library," said the Librarian. "Somewhere in those books I am sure to find the answer. But it may take many years."

"Begin at once then," said the King. "We have no time to lose!"

And so the Princess was laid in a bed in a high tower and a young soldier was set by her side to guard her. The Prince was placed in a pond in the castle garden where a young kitchen-maid was sent to look after him. As for the Librarian, he shut himself in the library and began to study the books, searching for the spell that would release the royal twins from their enchantment.

Long years passed. The young soldier sat in the tower and sang songs to the sleeping Princess and she heard him in her dreams and smiled as she slept. The little kitchen-maid brought food to the Frog-Prince and stroked his knobbly head with stalks of grass while he sat in her hand and blinked at her. And as the Princess grew older she grew more beautiful so that the young soldier fell in love with her. And though the Prince did not grow handsomer as he grew older the kitchen-maid got used to his ugliness so that she grew to love him also.

Finally, one day when fifteen years had passed, the Librarian entered the throne room where the King and Queen were sitting. His back was bent from long years of poring over books and his eyes were weak and watery from long nights of reading by candlelight. But on his face he wore a tired smile.

"Sire," he said, "I have found the answer!"

"Where?" asked the King in amazement.

"In here," said the Librarian, holding up a book.

"The Frog Prince, the Sleeping Beauty and Other Favourite Tales," read the King. "And this book has the answer?"

"Yes, sire," said the Librarian, and opening the book he read in a loud voice:

"SLEEP LIKE DEATH THE OLD KING'S DAUGHTER
OLD KING'S SON SHALL DWELL IN WATER
FOREVER THIS SPELL LASTS UNLESS
THEY'RE KISSED BY PRINCE AND BY PRINCESS."

"I could have told you that!" said the Court Astrologer.

"KISS AND WAKE UP!" scribbled the editor of the *Daily Dragon*.

"Summon every prince and princess in the land," cried the King joyfully. "Tell them that the ones who break this spell shall be married to my son and daughter!"

A few days later, the King and Queen sat in the throne room looking at the great crowd of princes and princesses who had gathered there, hoping to be the ones to break the spell and marry into the Royal Family.

"Just look at the state of them!" said the King gloomily. "Ridiculous powdered wigs, faces covered in make-up, and as for those *hideous* tights!"

"Yes, dear," said the Queen. "And the princesses are even worse!"

A sudden silence fell as the doors opened and the young soldier strode into the hall carrying the sleeping Princess in his arms. Behind him came the little kitchen-maid with the Frog-Prince squatting and blinking in her hand.

"Gad, what a scrawny little gel!" drawled one of the princes. "I hope she doesn't have bedsores! Wot? Wot?"

"Does one really have to kiss that horrid frog?" brayed a princess. "One hopes it doesn't give one warts!"

The soldier and the kitchen-maid stood before the throne.

The kitchen-maid hung her head and a tear trickled from her eye, but the soldier looked proudly at the King and spoke in a strong voice.

"Sire," he said, "we are but humble servants of Your Majesty. But for fifteen years we have watched over your children. And now we have a favour to ask."

"Ask it," said the King.

"Before we give them up to their royal destiny . . ." said the soldier.

"We should like to kiss them goodbye," said the little kitchen-maid in a terrified whisper.

"Egad, dashed impertinence!" drawled a prince. "I've a good mind to punch that fellow on the nose!"

"Commoners kissing royalty!" brayed a princess. "They'll be wanting to marry us next!"

"Silence!" thundered the King. Then he smiled at the soldier and the kitchen-maid. "Your favour is granted," he said.

"Well, really!" brayed a princess.

"It weminds one of the worst excesses of the Fwench Wevolution!" drawled a prince.

The soldier bent and kissed the sleeping Princess and a great gasp went up from the watching crowd. For as soon as his lips touched hers she blinked and woke and smiled at him.

"I thought you were only a dream," she said.

At the same time the kitchen-maid kissed the Frog-Prince.

This time there came an even louder gasp and several princesses screamed and fainted. For the frog had vanished and there, standing hand in hand with the kitchen-maid, was a handsome young prince, dripping wet and totally naked! The Librarian hastily covered him with a cloak. ("PRINCE DISPLAYS FAMILY JEWELS!" scribbled the editor of the *Daily Dragon*, wishing that photography had been invented.)

"Well, that's that," said the King, ignoring the outraged protests of the watching princes and princesses. "They broke the spell so they marry my son and daughter."

"But, sire," said the Royal Librarian, "he's a soldier and she's a kitchen-maid. They are not of royal blood!"

"If this kitchen-maid marries my son she'll be a princess, yes?" said the King.

"Well, yes, sire," said the Librarian.

"And if this soldier marries my daughter he'll be a prince?" asked the King.

"Well, strictly speaking . . ." began the Librarian.

"I knew you'd agree with me," said the King. "So now it's all settled."

"I predict they will all live happily ever after!" said the Court Astrologer.

"That's what all the books say, anyway!" said the Royal Librarian.

"Well, I hope you're wrong," said the editor of the *Daily Dragon*.

"Why do you say that?" asked the King in astonishment.

"I'll tell you why I say it, sire," said the editor gloomily. "Because happy endings don't make headlines!"

THE ADVENTURES OF TOM SAWYER

MARK TWAIN

First published in 1876, The Adventures of Tom Sawyer *is a classic story, and its hero a much-loved comic character. In this extract Tom uses all his resources to avoid school. Perhaps something everyone has been tempted to do on a Monday morning!*

MONDAY MORNING found Tom Sawyer miserable. Monday morning always found him so – because it began another week's slow suffering in school. He generally began that day with wishing he had had no intervening holiday, it made the going into captivity and fetters again so much more odious.

Tom lay thinking. Presently it occurred to him that he wished he was sick; then he could stay home from school. Here was a vague possibility. He canvassed his system. No ailment was found, and he investigated again. This time he thought he could detect colicky symptoms, and he began to encourage them with considerable hope. But they soon grew feeble, and presently died wholly away. He reflected further. Suddenly he discovered something. One of his upper front teeth was loose. This was lucky; he was about to begin to groan, as a "starter", as he called it, when it occurred to him that if he came into court with that argument, his aunt would pull it out, and that would hurt. So he thought he would hold the tooth in reserve for the present, and seek further. Nothing offered for some little time, and then he remembered hearing the doctor tell about a certain thing that laid up a patient for two or three weeks and threatened to make him lose a finger. So the boy eagerly drew his sore toe from under the sheet and held it up for inspection. But now he did not know the necessary symptoms. However, it seemed well worthwhile to chance it, so he fell to groaning with considerable spirit.

But Sid slept on unconscious.

Tom groaned louder, and fancied that he began to feel pain in the toe.

No result from Sid.

Tom was panting with his exertions by this time. He took a rest and then swelled himself up and fetched a succession of admirable groans.

Sid snored on.

Tom was aggravated. He said, "Sid, Sid!" and shook him. This course worked well, and Tom began to groan again. Sid yawned, stretched, then brought himself up on his elbow with a snort, and began to stare at Tom. Tom went on groaning. Sid said:

"Tom! Say, Tom!" [No response.] "Here, Tom! Tom! What is the matter, Tom?" And he shook him and looked in his face anxiously.

Tom moaned out:

"Oh, don't, Sid. Don't joggle me."

"Why, what's the matter, Tom? I must call Auntie."

"No – never mind. It'll be over by and by, maybe. Don't call anybody."

"But I must! Don't groan so, Tom, it's awful. How long you been this way?"

"Hours. Ouch! Oh, don't stir so, Sid, you'll kill me."

"Tom, why didn't you wake me sooner? Oh, Tom, don't! It makes my flesh crawl to hear you. Tom, what is the matter?"

"I forgive you everything, Sid. [Groan.] Everything you've ever done to me. When I'm gone –"

"Oh, Tom, you ain't dying, are you? Don't, Tom – oh, don't. Maybe –"

"I forgive everybody, Sid. [Groan.] Tell 'em so, Sid. And Sid, you give my window sash and my cat with one eye to that new girl that's come to town, and tell her –"

But Sid had snatched his clothes and gone. Tom was suffering in reality, now, so handsomely was his imagination working, and so his groans had gathered quite a genuine tone.

Sid flew downstairs and said:

"Oh, Aunt Polly, come! Tom's dying!"

"Dying!"

"Yes'm. Don't wait – come quick!"

"Rubbage! I don't believe it!"

But she fled upstairs, nevertheless, with Sid and Mary at her heels. And her face grew white, too, and her lip trembled. When she reached the bedside she gasped out:

"You Tom! Tom, what's the matter with you?"

"Oh, Auntie, I'm –"

"What's the matter with you – what is the matter with you, child?"

"Oh, Auntie, my sore toe's mortified!"

The old lady sank down into a chair and laughed a little, then cried a little, then did both together. This restored her and she said:

"Tom, what a turn you did give me. Now you shut up that nonsense and climb out of this."

The groans ceased and the pain vanished from the toe. The boy felt a little foolish, and he said:

"Aunt Polly, it seemed mortified, and it hurt so I never minded my tooth at all."

"Your tooth, indeed! What's the matter with your tooth?"

"One of them's loose, and it aches perfectly awful."

"There, there, now, don't begin that groaning again. Open your mouth. Well – your tooth is loose, but you're not going to die about that. Mary, get me a silk thread, and a chunk of fire out of the kitchen."

Tom said:

"Oh, please, Auntie, don't pull it out. It don't hurt any more. I wish I may never stir if it does. Please don't, Auntie. I don't want to stay home from school."

"Oh, you don't, don't you? So all this row was because you thought you'd get to stay home from school and go a-fishing? Tom, Tom, I love you so, and you seem to try every way you can to break my old heart with your outrageousness." By this time the dental instruments were ready. The old lady made one end of the silk thread fast to Tom's tooth with a loop and tied the other to the bedpost. Then she seized the chunk of fire and suddenly thrust it almost into the boy's face. The tooth hung dangling by the bedpost, now.

But all trials bring their compensations. As Tom wended to school after breakfast, he was the envy of every boy he met because the gap in his upper row of teeth enabled him to expectorate in a new and admirable way. He gathered quite a following of lads interested in the exhibition; and one that had cut his finger and had been a centre of fascination and homage up to this time, now found himself suddenly without an adherent, and shorn of his glory. His heart was heavy, and he said with a disdain which he did not feel, that it wasn't anything to spit like Tom Sawyer; but another boy said, "Sour grapes!" and he wandered away a dismantled hero.

THE GREAT GOLDEN BELLY-BUTTON

MICHAEL ROSEN

KING JABBER sat listening to the concert. The Ding-a-ling Brothers were singing their song, "If I was a pudding, I'd ask you to be the custard". Oh dear, it was the thirty-ninth time he'd heard it and he hadn't liked it the first time. Yawn, yawn, yawn.

Then Donk the jester came on and told jokes. They were all terrible – especially the one about the pig that ate the King's underpants.

When Wizzo the wizard stood on the stage and said that he was going to take a rabbit and a donkey out of his hat, enough was enough. King Jabber stood up and said, "I can't stand any more of this rubbish. I want fun, I want laughter, I want . . . I want . . . egg on toast."

The entertainers hurried off the stage and Bradstock brought in the egg on toast. The toast was soggy. The egg was burnt. Or was it the other way round?

"I'm supposed to be the king around here," said Jabber. "I'm royal and regal and you're loyal and legal. I'm supposed to sit about and do nothing all day, you're supposed to be really glad you've got a king, even though I cost an enormous amount of money, and we're all supposed to be terribly, terribly happy. But what happens? I'm bored and the Ding-a-ling Brothers are still singing that stupid song about the pudding and the custard. What am I going to do, Bradstock?"

"First of all, sir, can I suggest that you wipe the egg off your chin? And then might I remind you, sir, of the Great Golden Belly-button you had made?"

"Yes, yes, yes, Bradstock. I do remember. What of it?"

"Well, sir," said Bradstock, "you don't seem to have found much use for it yet."

"Use? Use? You don't use a Great Golden Belly-button. It just is. I had it made because it's a good sight more fun than listening to Wizzo, Donk and the Ding-a-lings."

"I understand, sir," said Bradstock, "but I would like to suggest that you give it away as a kind of prize. Whoever can make you laugh the most, will win the Great Golden Belly-button."

"No, Bradstock anyone can make me laugh. It's too easy. I've got a better idea. Whoever can tell the biggest lie will win the Great Golden Belly-button. How about that?"

"Excellent idea, sir!"

So the herald went out all around the country telling people: "Hear this! Hear this! Whoever can show themselves to be the biggest liar in all the land will receive the Great Golden Belly-button from the hands of King Jabber himself."

It wasn't long before the palace was packed with people telling lies.

There was the woman who said she had a horse that could say, "sausages"; the man who said he had grass growing in his armpits; the woman who said she could swallow armchairs, and so on and so on.

Once again, King Jabber was getting bored.

"It's time we ended this stupid game of yours, Bradstock."

"Your stupid game, sir."

"Yours!"

"Yours!"

"Yours!"

Just then a voice piped up, "I'm here."

Bradstock and King Jabber looked round, and there stood a small girl with a bowl in her hand.

"Who are you?" asked the King.

"Oh, come on," said the girl, whose name was Peggy. "You remember me, don't you? You owe me a hundred gold pieces. I've come to collect them in my bowl here. It did have cornflakes in, but it's clean now."

"A hundred gold pieces? A hundred gold pieces?" said the King. "I've never seen you before in my life. I've never promised you any money and you're a liar to say I have."

"You promised. You did!"

"Did you hear that, Bradstock? Have you ever heard a liar like this little sprat? Get out of here, girl, before I set my dogs on you."

"Just hold it right there," said Peggy. "If you've never heard a liar like me before, then you must give me the Great Golden Belly-button."

"Ah. Er, well. Er, no . . ." said the King. "Of course I didn't mean you were really a liar, I, er . . ."

"Oh well, if I'm not a liar then give me my hundred pieces of gold," said Peggy.

There was a silence. Bradstock waited to be given the order to set the dogs on her.

"Well sock me sideways, the little sprat has done it!" said King Jabber. "Girl, the Great Golden Belly-button is yours. Give it to her, Bradstock."

Bradstock gave Peggy the Belly-button and she left the palace with it in her breakfast bowl.

"Stupid game you thought up there," said the King to Bradstock.

"Stupid game you thought up, sir," said Bradstock.

"No *you* thought up."

"No *you* thought up."

"*You* thought up."

"More egg on toast, sir?"

"I suppose so," said the King.

THE RATCATCHER

ERROL LLOYD

ONCE UPON A TIME there was a farmer whose farmhouse was over-run with rats. There were rats everywhere. In the loft, under the floorboards, in the cupboards, in the larder. They were even in the bedrooms. But what was even worse was that they were in the granary where he stored his grain and they were eating out his winter's supply of corn and barley.

"These rats will be my ruin," he said. "I must get rid of them at all costs."

So he set traps baited with the finest cheese, he put down horrible poison, and he even got several cats, but nothing seemed to work. The rats always found a way to set off the trap then eat up the cheese; and somehow they seemed to learn very quickly how to identify the poison and avoid eating it; and even if the cats managed to catch any rats they never caught enough to make any difference, for the rats continued to thrive and increase in numbers.

Eventually the farmer became so desperate that he put an advertisement in the evening paper offering a reward to any ratcatcher who could get rid of the rats.

The next evening a ratcatcher, dressed in a suit and hat and carrying a briefcase, knocked on the farmer's door.

"I don't suppose you are the ratcatcher?" said the farmer, looking him over.

"I am the regional pest control operative," said the ratcatcher, who did not like to be called a ratcatcher.

"Yes, but do you catch rats?" inquired the farmer in a gruff voice, for he was never one for big words.

"I specialize in rodents," said the ratcatcher, "and that includes rodents of the genus rattus."

"Yes, but do you blinkin' catch rats?" shrieked the farmer, who was beginning to lose all patience with the ratcatcher.

"I have been known to catch rats in large numbers," said the ratcatcher, "and I have come in answer to your advertisement in the newspaper."

"Where is your equipment then?" asked the farmer, who thought it a very odd ratcatcher indeed who didn't wear a white boiler suit and travel with a van full of equipment.

"I have just about everything I need here," said the ratcatcher, patting the side of his briefcase.

Before the farmer could say anything, his wife, who had been standing behind him, intervened: "Aren't you going to invite in the rat . . . er, the, er, regional . . ."

"The regional pest control operative," offered the ratcatcher, taking off his hat and bowing to the lady. "Thank you kindly, madam," he said. "Most generous of you." And with that he swept through the door and into the front room.

Before long he was settled in a seat in front of the fire drinking a cup of warm tea, which the farmer's wife had brewed up for him, and eating cake that she had baked that very day.

While the ratcatcher drank his tea and ate his cake, the farmer had a good look at his briefcase. "I don't know what you have in that briefcase," he said, "but whatever it is, I must warn you that there are hundreds of rats here, and you won't be paid a penny unless you kill every last one of them."

"It is not my policy to kill rats or any other living creature," replied the ratcatcher.

"I thought you came to get rid of the rats!" bellowed the farmer.

"That I intend to do," said the ratcatcher. "But without killing a single rat."

The farmer scratched his head.

"When do you intend to start?" he asked, as bad-temperedly as ever.

"We can discuss the details after dinner," said the ratcatcher.

"Dinner!" shrieked the farmer. He was just about to explode when his wife again hurried to smooth things over.

"Of course you must have dinner with us," she said. "After all, you can't be expected to catch rats on an empty stomach now, can you?"

"Indeed not, madam," said the ratcatcher, reaching for a second slice of cake. "Indeed not!"

After a typical wholesome farm dinner of beef stew with carrots, dumplings and potatoes, washed down with home-made ale and followed by apple-pie and custard, the ratcatcher retired to the comfort of the easy chair beside the fire (which, unknown to him, was the farmer's chair), where he had his coffee. After coffee he lit up his pipe and puffed away contentedly.

The peace and quiet of the rustic scene was broken only by the occasional sound of rats scurrying about in the ceiling above and under the floorboards below.

"When are you going to start, then?" inquired the farmer, even more impatiently than before.

"I shall start on the dot of five o'clock when I wake in the morning," replied the ratcatcher, suppressing a yawn.

"In the morning!" bellowed the farmer.

"So you'll be sleeping overnight then?" inquired the farmer's wife, for though she too was becoming somewhat impatient with the fellow she knew the desperate plight they were in with the rats and didn't want to upset him.

"Just a simple bed will do," said the ratcatcher. "Nothing too fancy." He then went on to explain that as the rats only came out of hiding after dark, he could only work during the hours of darkness.

"I suppose you can sleep in the guest room," said the farmer's wife. "It's the first door on the left upstairs."

"Thank you kindly, madam," said the ratcatcher.

"Mind you," added the farmer's wife, "there are probably lots of rats that go in there during the night."

"That will suit me fine," said the ratcatcher, putting out his pipe and rising from the chair. "I have an early start in the morning so I had best retire now."

"Well, I hope you have a good night's sleep," said the farmer's wife.

"There's just one thing I require," said the ratcatcher, "and that's an empty bin." And he held his hands three feet from the floor to indicate how big it needed to be.

"We have just the thing," said the farmer's wife. She went to the kitchen and returned with a large plastic bin.

"I hope this will do," she said.

"Perfect," said the ratcatcher. "Absolutely perfect. By the time we have had breakfast tomorrow morning, there won't be a single rat in the house."

"Breakfast!" exploded the farmer.

"My favourite meal of the day," said the ratcatcher, and bowing to the farmer and his wife he bid them goodnight and retired to the guest room, carrying the plastic bin with him.

The farmer and his wife looked on somewhat mystified as he disappeared up the stairs.

Once in the bedroom the ratcatcher opened his briefcase and took out a pair of pyjamas, a ruler, a piece of cheese and a painting set. He placed the plastic bin near the bed. Then he rested one end of the ruler on the bedside table and carefully balanced the rest on the rim of the bin, so that the other end of the ruler hung over it, just like a diving board over a swimming pool. At this end he carefully placed a piece of cheese.

He then put on his pyjamas, turned off the light and went to sleep.

On the stroke of midnight, a rat squeezed through a hole in the corner of the guest room and silently crept in the direction of the bin, where there was a strong smell of cheese. He climbed onto the top of the briefcase and from here clambered onto the bedside table, from where he saw the bit of cheese at the tip of the ruler.

He cautiously stepped onto the ruler and started to inch his way towards the cheese. Once he got to the rim of the bin the cheese was tantalizingly near. He edged towards it, but before he could reach the cheese the weight of his body tipped the ruler forwards, and ruler, cheese and rat fell headlong into the bin.

The sides of the bin were too slippery for the rat to climb and the bin too deep for him to jump out, either. He was trapped.

As if by long habit, the ratcatcher woke promptly at five o'clock in the morning. He got out of bed and set to work immediately. He got out the painting set and clutching the rat between his thumb and index finger he painted its tail a brilliant emerald green. He then painted white zebra-like stripes along the side of the rat; its legs he painted a deep purple; finally he painted its face a fluorescent yellow, before adding a series of pink polka dots. As a finishing touch he painted the rat's nose a bright red, just like a clown's.

He then took the rat over to the hole in the corner of the room.

"Don't worry, my little friend," he said. "The next downpour of rain will wash this off and you will be back to normal."

He then released the rat and got back into bed.

The rat disappeared down the hole and dashed off as fast as his purple legs could carry him, back towards the communal home he shared with the other rats. But when the other rats saw this strange creature running at full speed towards them, with a red nose, a yellow face with pink polka dots, and with white stripes down its side and a green tail, there was panic and pandemonium. Rats shrieked and fled in every direction. They ran out of the attic, out from under the floorboards, out from behind cupboards and from every nook and cranny in which they were hiding. The painted rat, who couldn't see himself, had no idea why they were running away and ran even faster to catch up. This made the other rats even more terrified and they ran away all the faster.

They ran down the staircase, down the passage and in a mad rush they charged through the cat flap. They ran through the granary, where they frightened more rats, and from there they fled into the fields. And all the time they were still being

pursued by the multi-coloured rat, who still couldn't understand why they were all running away from him.

That morning over breakfast, which consisted of porridge, bacon and eggs and sausages, thick slices of toast and marmalade, and tea, the farmer and his wife thanked the ratcatcher heartily. They were overjoyed at having got rid of the rats.

"You have saved us," said the farmer.

"Have more toast and marmalade," said the farmer's wife. "You must be ever so hungry after all that work."

"Nothing to it," said the ratcatcher modestly, spreading mounds of marmalade onto a thick slice of toast.

"You must let us know how much we have to pay you," said the farmer. "No price is too high after what you have done for us."

"You needn't worry about money," said the ratcatcher. "There is no charge."

"But there must be something we can do for you," said the farmer.

"My needs are few," said the ratcatcher. "As I go from house to house offering my services, I always get invited to tea and dinner and I get a bed for the night and breakfast in the morning. The only worry I have is lunch. So there you have it, sir. If you want to reward me, then reward me with lunch."

"You'll have the best lunch you ever had in your life," said the farmer.

"Thank you most kindly," said the ratcatcher. "Now you can see why breakfast is my favourite meal. It's usually during breakfast that I get offered the best meal of my life!"

And that is how the ratcatcher came to have a most sumptuous lunch with the farmer and his wife before moving on to his next job that evening.

AT THE ZOO

BRIAN PATTEN

TWO NEW CREATURES had arrived at the zoo, and Class 10XA were clustered around the cage, studying them.

"Don't go so near the cage," said the teacher.

"They don't look dangerous," said one of the pupils.

"They look sweet," said another.

"They might look sweet," said the teacher, "but that's because they are young, and even the young ones are known to be quite vicious at times. They are carnivorous from a very early age, remember."

"What's carnivorous?" asked one of the pupils.

"It means they eat meat."

"Does that mean they would eat us?"

"Quite possibly," said the teacher.

"They look tame," said another pupil. "They've hardly moved since we came."

"That's because they are more interested in the box in the corner of their cage than in us, I suspect," said the teacher.

"If you put one of those boxes in front of them, they will sit for hours. It's when you take the box away that they go a bit wild."

"Well, I think they are very sweet," said one of the class.

"They look slightly like the monkeys in the other cage. Are they as intelligent?"

"Oh, no," said the teacher. "They can't do half the things the monkeys can."

"I think they are quite boring myself," said another of the pupils, "and all that pink skin – yuk! They're so ugly!"

"Maybe they'd be more interesting if they weren't gaping at that box," said the teacher.

"But they do move about, usually in the daylight. Anyway, they are part of our zoo project, and you must all use your computer notepads to describe them."

Class 10XA soon got bored looking at the new arrivals and moved along to another cage.

As they drifted away, one of the pupils asked, "Where did you say they came from?"

"I've already told you," said the teacher. "Honestly, Harsog! Sometimes I think you've no brains in any of your three heads! They are from a planet called Earth, and they are called children. Now, don't let me have to tell you again!"

JULIUS CAESAR'S GOAT

DICK KING-SMITH

Dick King-Smith is famous for his animal characters. This extract recounts Caesar's first meeting with the star of this story: a magnificent, pongy goat.

YOU MIGHT THINK you knew quite a bit about Julius Caesar. I bet you didn't know that he had absolutely no sense of smell.

Though his parents were not all that bright – his father's name was Crassus Idioticus and his mother was called Stupida – Julius was in fact a quick-witted boy, with excellent hearing and twenty-twenty vision, but from the age of ten onwards he couldn't smell a thing. He couldn't smell bread baking or meat roasting, and the scent of flowers meant nothing to him.

It happened like this.

Julius, who had been born in the year 100 BC, was playing with a lot of other boys in the playground at North Rome Primary School. It was 15 March (the Ides of March, the Romans called it) 90 BC and they were playing with a large, round ball made from a cow's stomach packed with scraps of rags from old togas.

The game was called Foot-the-Ball, and the idea was to kick it between two posts. The only person allowed to touch the ball with his hands was called the Keeper of the Goal, and that is what Caesar was that particular morning.

There was a great flurry in the mouth of the goal and one of Julius's opponents, a rough boy called Brutus, took a spectacular overhead kick at the ball and missed it. His foot hit Julius smack on the nose.

"Et tu, Brute!" cried Julius (which, loosely translated, means "It would be you, you brute!") and he retired, hurt.

Stupida was horrified when her son arrived home, his handsome Roman nose all swollen – so swollen, in fact, that even Crassus Idioticus noticed.

But the swelling went down and Julius's nose looked much as it had before, apart from a slight bend in the middle. But it didn't work. Julius Caesar had lost his sense of smell, forever.

They took him to all the best medical men in Rome, sparing no expense, but none could help, though one, the oldest and wisest, said to Julius, "You must count your blessings, young man. The world may be full of pleasant smells, but it is also filled with horrible stinks and stenches, which now will never worry you."

Julius Caesar never forgot this wise old man's remark, and many years later, when he was already a famous soldier, he used his handicap to great advantage.

In 49 BC he was commanding an army in Gaul and decided to attack another army led by a man called Pompey. To do this, he had to cross a stream called the Rubicon.

On the banks of this stream was a herd of goats, which Caesar's legionaries, always eager for fresh meat, killed quickly and butchered. Amongst the nanny goats was one very large billy goat with long ginger hair and a pair of fine sweeping horns which broke free from the slaughterers and ran, bleating loudly, towards Julius Caesar himself as he strode down to the water's edge, surrounded by his bodyguard.

Hastily the bodyguard drew back because of the appalling smell that the billy goat gave out. All billy goats stink, but this one was a champion stinker.

Then a brave centurion stepped forward. "O Caesar!" he cried.

146

"Wilt thou have this beast for lunch?" and he waited, sword upraised, his eyes on his leader's right hand.

If Caesar's thumb had then been turned down, one swipe would have removed the animal's head from its body.

Caesar looked down at the billy goat. He was impressed by the look in its eyes, a look much more intelligent than that of Crassus Idioticus or Stupida.

Meanwhile, the watching soldiers marvelled. There was Caesar, standing right by the stinking creature, even laying his hand upon its head!

"O great Caesar!" they whispered to each other. "What courage!"

Little did they know that he couldn't smell a thing.

Still the brave centurion waited, his sword upraised, holding his nose with the other hand.

Then Caesar said, "*Hircus audens est*" (which, loosely translated, means, "That goat's got bottle"), and he put his thumb up.

The centurion lowered his sword, and Julius Caesar, closely followed by his goat, waded into the water and crossed the Rubicon.

Now, as his legions prepared to march south to confront the army of Pompey, Caesar issued an edict with regard to his new pet. Caesar's goat was to be accorded all possible honour, and anyone found guilty of treating it with disrespect would be put to death. As for the man who would have executed the animal if the general's thumb had turned down, he, much to his dismay, was appointed Centurion-Capricorn. Not even a rise in pay of one *denarius per diem* could compensate him for having now to live permanently in close proximity to that awful pong, but of course he could not complain.

"*Caesus durus!*" his mates whispered to him (which, loosely translated, means "Hard cheese!").

Now, as the legions moved south, Julius Caesar and his bodyguard, along with the Centurion-Capricorn and the animal itself, marched in the middle of the column of soldiers. The wind was in the north and thus blew upon their backs. It was a strong wind, so all those marching behind Caesar were in luck, for they were spared the smell of the billy goat. All those ahead of Caesar, however, caught the full impact of the wind-borne stink.

But then someone among those forward troops had a brilliant idea.

"If only that goat marched in front of us," he said, "right at the head of the column, the wind would carry the smell away from us too."

Then someone else had an even more brilliant idea.

"What if Pompey's army were ahead of us? If we were free of the stink and they were being suffocated by it? Why, before they'd recovered from the shock, we could make mincemeat of them!"

"By Jupiter! They'd all be gasping and choking, like we are now, and their eyes would be running, like ours are now, and they wouldn't be able to fight for toffee!"

"Yes, but how can we persuade Caesar to put the brute at the head of the army? 'Why?' he'd say, and we couldn't say, 'Because it stinks so bad.' That'd be disrespect and we'd be topped."

"What can we do then?"

"I know!" said a smarmy little legionary called Oleaginus. "Leave it to me. I'll fix it."

That night when they set up camp, Oleaginus made his way to Julius Caesar's tent to crave an audience with the general.

He found Caesar feeding his goat, while behind him stood the Centurion-Capricorn, holding a fold of his toga discreetly over his nose.

"What is it, soldier?" said the general.

"O great Caesar!" said Oleaginus in his oiliest voice. "I come with a request from all my fellow legionaries."

"A request? What about?"

"About that most beautiful of creatures, Your Excellency's goat."

"What about it?"

"O great Caesar!" said Oleaginus. "If only this noble animal could lead us into battle! How the sight of it, at the head of the army, would inspire every man behind it, while at the same time striking terror into the hearts of Your Excellency's foes!"

149

"D'you really think so?" said Caesar.

"Truly, O great Caesar!" replied Oleaginus in a choking voice, his eyes streaming, for the stench of the billy goat in the confined space of the tent was overpowering.

Ye Gods! thought Caesar, observing the legionary's tears. The poor fellow's overcome with emotion. Already my men have come to think of my goat as a mascot. With him to lead them, they'll fight like lions!

So it was that when Caesar's army struck camp next morning to continue the southward march, the north wind still at their backs, the two leading figures in the long column of soldiers were the Centurion-Capricorn and the goat.

When at long last the two opposing armies met, they would have seemed to an observer to be equally matched. On either side were three legions, each of 3,000 men. Within each legion were ten cohorts, each of 300 men. Within each cohort were three centuries, each of 100 men.

But it was an ill wind that blew in the faces of Pompey's army that day, for it carried upon it a thick, choking, acrid smell, before which Pompey's leading troops began first to falter and then to turn away in panic, rank after rank pushing and shoving back through their fellows in an effort to escape that ghastly miasma, until at last the whole army turned tail in a wild stampede.

The history books may well tell you that Caesar defeated Pompey in the civil war between those two generals.

Rubbish!

Pompey and his legions were routed by Julius Caesar's goat.

VIKING TREASURE

ROGER McGOUGH

This story is taken from my own collection The Stowaways. *Just after the end of the Second World War the beaches around Liverpool were exciting but dangerous places on which to play . . .*

ONE THURSDAY MORNING, straight after Assembly, the school was raided by Vikings. Fierce men with red beards, waving heavy swords and axes, suddenly emerged from the back of the hall, and ran between the rows of innocent children, yelling and clanking. Of course, they didn't fool me for a minute. Real Viking warriors, I knew, wouldn't wear false beards (or, worse still, be seen dead in yellow and blue trainers). But they were convincing enough to make most of the kids scream and get excited, until the headmaster quietened everybody down and introduced the theatre group. (Two of the fiercest-looking warriors, by the way, turned out to be girls, which just goes to show what a big helmet and a blood-stained axe can do for you.)

They all said hello, and told us that they were touring the schools on Merseyside performing a play about life in Liverpool when the Vikings arrived, thousands of years ago. It was really interesting to learn, not only about the Viking invaders but about the Anglo-Saxons who had lived in the area and the Romans

151

who came later to set up their garrisons. I looked with new eyes at the kids around me and could imagine them as the children of Saxon farmers or Roman soldiers and suddenly they all seemed more interesting.

That Thursday morning was one of the best times I ever had in school, and made ordinary lessons seem boring. Midge agreed, although what really excited him was the thought of being an actor. What he intended to do when he grew up, he said, was to be a member of a theatre group which visited schools and chased children with large swords. I had to agree that to be an adult and get paid for dressing-up and playing soldiers seemed as good a job as there was.

A week later came half-term. It was October, and a bullying one. It wore a grey frown and kicked the leaves about. It shook the trees and it banged on the window-panes. But it was mainly bravado. (The real tough guys, Jan and Feb, could be really mean when they wanted to. No sooner is Christmas over than they are holed up in the sky like besieged gangsters, armed with snow bullets and winds tipped with ice.)

October may be loud-mouthed, but it's usually dry. So Midge and I were able to go out every day, either playing footy in the park, with other lads who lived nearby, or taking Bunker for long runs along the canal bank.

The days sped by happily enough, but on Friday we felt like doing something different, and Midge had the idea of getting the train out to Formby and then walking back along the shore. "What we need before we go back to school," he said, "is buckets full of sea air."

So, at about ten o'clock, we set off, our rucksacks stacked with corned-beef sandwiches, dog biscuits and pop; and an hour later we were heading into the hilly sand dunes that range along the shore north from Liverpool. Once you cross through the dunes you come to the flat beach that stretches out to the Irish Sea. Miles and miles of nothing but miles and miles. The hills of sand seemed to offer more fun. So, first things first: we sat on the tough grass on the highest dune we could find and ate our sarnies and drank our pop. (Bunker was too interested in chasing seagulls, so we saved his lunch for later.)

In summer, the place would have been chock-a-block with day-trippers and smooching couples, but that day, thanks to sullen October, we had the battlefield to ourselves.

At first, we were Viking raiders making mincemeat out of the Ancient Brits. Then, we were commandos, sneaking up on enemy soldiers and throwing grenades into their dugouts. Or charging down the sandy slopes, machine-guns blazing. Finally, when we had exhausted ourselves wiping out the German SS, two Roman legions, the entire Sioux nation and countless invaders from outer space, the three brave warriors (well two and a half really) headed down onto the shore and in the direction of home.

Ahead, in the far distance, we could see the twinkling lights, the giant cranes, and tower blocks of Liverpool. And above the city, a cloud of grey smoke hovered, like a bad mood. Across the river on the opposite side was Birkenhead, and pencilled faintly in behind, were the mountains of Wales.

But when we stopped to look straight out across the bottle-grey waters, where the River Mersey runs into the Irish Sea, no land could be seen. Only ships returning wearily to port, or setting out, spirits high, to see the world.

"Why don't we run away to sea again Midge, and this time do it properly?"

Midge shook his head. "Nah, I'm going to be an actor, then if I feel like going to sea I can get a part as a sailor in a film. That way you don't get seasick either."

"Oh, but it's not the same," I argued.

But Midge wouldn't have it.

"Anyway, you couldn't run away to sea now," he said, stooping to pick up a small piece of wood.

"Why not?" I asked. Instead of saying anything, Midge threw the stick into the waves that rolled noisily onto the sand.

The answer to my question bounded joyfully in to fetch it. Of course, Bunker. I could hardly leave him. Mum and Dad would understand my going off in search of adventure – well, at least

I hoped they would – but not Bunker. There are some things you just can't explain to dogs.

In silence then we walked, and quickly, because we were tired and hungry, and home seemed a long way off.

Only Bunker was tireless as he streaked across the sand in all directions, flapping like a piece of black and white wind.

And it was Bunker of course who found the buried treasure.

He was sniffing around what looked like a small, black pyramid, and barking with an excitement that made us break into a run. As we drew nearer, we could see that it was a box, half buried in the sand. Having dumped it, the waves, now bored, were pulling away and going home to bed.

Needless to say, any thoughts we'd had of going home were now forgotten, as we scooped out the wet sand, and dug and tugged with the superhuman energy we saved for special occasions. Soon we were able to pull it free and look closely at our prize. It was a box of black, rusted metal, about the size of the chest that Long John Silver and the pirates fought over on Treasure Island.

For this was surely gold that had once belonged to the Vikings, so vivid were our memories of their school visit the week before. Perhaps, after a raid on Liverpool, one of their ships, laden with stolen treasure, had been wrecked by a storm, and now, hundreds of years later, the sea was giving away one of its dark secrets.

Midge and I dragged the box up the beach and away from the sea's clutches. We couldn't wait to open it and run our fingers through the heavy, gold coins, and try on the priceless crowns . . . To fling sapphires and rubies into the darkening air. Diamonds that would out-twinkle even the stars that were beginning to take root in the sky.

The trouble was, we couldn't get it open. There was no lock, but the lid was firmly sealed, and try as we might (we tried for ages) we couldn't prise it open even a fraction of a fraction of an inch. Of course, we didn't have the proper tools. What we were using were bricks and pieces of metal and wood that were lying around.

154

"A hammer and a chisel, that's what we need," I said.

Midge nodded, "Either that or a few sticks of dynamite." Bunker wagged his tail in agreement. (I suppose he thought the box would be full of Dog Treasure like juicy bones, crunchy biscuits and huge hunks of meat. As if.)

"Well, we're not going to be able to drag this all the way home," said Midge, "and we won't be able to come back tonight with a hammer and chisel. So what do we do?"

"What we do," I said, "is bury the box for now and then come back tomorrow with the proper tools."

Midge agreed. "But let's be careful where we bury it, so that we can find it again." We decided it would be safer to bury it in among the sand dunes and away from the beach, where our digging might attract attention.

The box was as heavy and awkward to move as a dead camel, and as the handles were stuck fast, we had to push, shove and drag it up and down the hills of shifting sand, until at last we lay panting, in what seemed like the ideal hiding place. It was a deep hollow, so secret and safe that no one would stumble across it in a million years. Except us of course. And to make sure that we could, Midge and I climbed the highest hill that overlooked it and, with our backs to the sea, took our bearings. It was almost dark now, but we could still make out the clump of pine trees to the left, a long, low building straight ahead (that seemed part of an airfield), and to the right, an unfastened necklace of bright yellow lamps that curved above a road and dwindled into the distance.

We dug a hole about two feet deep, heaved in the box and covered it with sand. To mark the spot exactly, we made the letter X using sticks, bricks, and the leftovers of summer's litter.

"X marks the spot," said Midge when at last we had finished. "Goodnight sweet treasure, see you in the morning."

Then we set off for home. It was cold now, and dark as a shadow's shadow. But we hardly noticed. We were rich, we were famous. No more going out to work for Mum and Dad. No more bus passes for Midge's gran. For Bunker, a fairy-tale kennel, with a lamp-post in every room and a bone-shaped swimming pool in the garden. We would buy ships to stowaway in, schools to play truant from.

In next to no time (which is no time at all) we were home.

Saturday did not turn out as planned. We had both got home so late the night before that the grown-ups were up the wall. I could always tell when my dad was pretending to be angry. He would put on his shouting voice and I would pretend to be sorry. But this time he was upset, I could tell, so was Mum. And his shouting voice was real because it came from deep inside.

As the treasure was going to be our big surprise, Midge and I couldn't give the real reason for staying out well after bedtime. I made up a fib about getting lost, said I was sorry for upsetting them (which I was) and then went quietly to bed.

Next day I wasn't allowed out at all. Midge called at around midday, but I told him to keep away and lie low until Sunday when, hopefully, all would be forgiven, if not forgotten. Sure enough it was. And as if to celebrate the fact, the sun came out, bright and bold as brass (as it usually does, the day before you go back to school).

During the night Midge had had a brilliant idea. The brilliant idea was for us to ride out to Formby on our bikes, open the box with a hammer and chisel, and either (a) bring back the booty in our cycle bags, or (b) rest the box (if we failed to open it) between the crossbars of both bikes and wheel it home. Brilliant.

As Bunker didn't have a bike to ride, he had to stay behind as Midge and I pedalled forth on our great adventure. It was a pleasant ride on the coast road that runs to Southport, with a fresh wind behind, pushing us along. Impatiently almost.

In no time at all (which is next to no time), we turned left off the main road, through Formby village, past the railway station and onto the track that leads down into the sandy hills. The going quickly became heavy, and the only way we could manage was to shoulder our bikes and stagger up and down the dunes until we reached the firmer sand near the sea. There we remounted and cycled slowly in search of the spot where Bunker had first discovered the box.

We half hoped that the footprints we had left on Friday would be still waiting for us, eager to show us the way. But no such luck. The sea, the old sneak-thief, had nipped in overnight and taken them. (As I cycled, I wondered what the sea did with all those footprints, stolen from the shore. On the ocean floor somewhere, are they all neatly piled up waiting for their owners to come and collect them?)

We stopped when we thought we recognized the part of the beach where the box had been washed up, and turned left into the sand dunes. Following what we hoped was the path we had taken. Once more, we humped the bikes onto our shoulders and staggered up and down the hills in search of the spot marked X.

Being a Sunday afternoon, and sunny into the bargain, there were quite a few people about: joggers, dog walkers, lads playing football. They must have thought us very odd.

After ten minutes of slithering and sliding, we collapsed into two tangled heaps. "Whose brilliant idea was it to bring the bikes?" I said. Midge looked glum.

"They're slowing us down too much, and we can't leave them anywhere in case they get pinched."

Midge shook some sand out of his ear and said nothing. Then his face lit up: "I've got a brilliant idea. Why don't we bury the bikes here, mark the spot with an X, and then when we've found the box, come back and dig them up. Brilliant." I looked at him to see if he was being serious.

"Are you being serious?" I asked. His face broke into a grin. The idea of our spending hours and hours searching for buried bikes was so crazy that I jumped on him and tried to push his face into the sand, but couldn't for laughing. We rolled around then, fighting and giggling until at last we lay on our backs, dizzy and panting. The sky spun slowly round and round.

"If only we had a helicopter," I said, "we'd find the treasure in a couple of minutes."

"But we haven't," said Midge, "so it's no use thinking about it."

I sat up. "Let's start again, but this time we'll take it in turns. One looks after the bikes while the other searches."

And that's just what we did. For hours. The one minding the bikes sat on the beach, where he could easily be seen, while the other went inland and did the search. But not only were we unable to find the X, we couldn't even recognize the landmarks we had noted to give us our bearings. There were clumps of pine trees everywhere and lots of low buildings in the distance, with roads running in all directions.

Everything looked so different in the afternoon light. And of course, we couldn't wait until it got dark. Not with all the trouble we had caused on Friday. So, with heavy hearts and heavy shoes (which were full of sand – the shoes, that is, not the hearts), we cycled home.

The ride back was murder. We were now cycling against a wind that seemed determined not to let us get past. Most of the journey was spent in silence, heads down, legs that ached, pumping away.

As we neared Litherland, however, the wind stood aside and let us through. Able to sit upright on our saddles for the first time, and get our breath back, I suggested to Midge that we should tell the grown-ups about the treasure. We were back at school the next day, so it was important that they were let into the secret. My dad could organize a proper search party, using friends from work. He might even be able to fly a helicopter. Midge agreed that under the circumstances it made good sense. And so, as soon as we got back to ours, we told Mum and Dad the whole story.

When we had finished telling them, we probably thought that Dad would smile proudly and shake our hands, and that Mum would hug and kiss us, tears of joy streaming down her cheeks.

"What clever boys!" they would say "Discovering Viking treasure, and making us all richer than our wildest dreams. What clever, clever boys!"

But it wasn't like that. Not like that at all. Mum went pale and Dad began shouting. It wasn't the kind of shouting that came from deep inside. It was the sort that he put on when he wanted you to pay attention. The shouting didn't last long, but the lecture that followed it did. It was all about poisons and chemicals and explosives. And about how, when he was a boy, one of his friends had had his hand blown off when opening a box found on the beach. There are horrible accidents, even worse than that, every year, he said.

When he had finished, Midge and I were paler than Mum. Then Midge had another of his "brilliant" ideas: "Maybe if we told the police, we might get a reward."

For the first time that evening, Dad smiled. "There wouldn't be any reward, I'm afraid, but you could report it to the police. The problem would be finding it. You see, those sand dunes may look like miniature mountains but they're not. They are made out of sand and they shift and move whenever the wind blows. The X that you made will have vanished forever. And the box? Well it may turn up again one day. And if it does, let's hope that whoever finds it has got more sense than you two. Viking treasure indeed!"

The next day was school again as usual, and we heard no more about the box after that. There was nothing on television about explosions on Formby beach. No reports of Viking treasure being discovered. It must be buried still beneath the sand. That box of dark secrets, impatient to be opened.

BREAK A LEG

JOEL SCHWARTZ

I WOULDN'T HAVE GONE to the "Getting to Know You" dance at
school if it hadn't been for my father. He wouldn't have talked
to me about it if it hadn't been for my mother. She wouldn't
have talked to him about it if it hadn't been for my best friend
Myron's mother. My best friend's mother wouldn't have talked to
my mother about it if it hadn't been for my best friend Myron.
Myron wouldn't have talked to his mother about it if I hadn't
talked to him about it, so I guess I'm to blame for everything.

It's not that I don't like dances and it's certainly not that
I don't like girls. It's just that, well, all the twelve-year-old girls
in the world are much taller than all the twelve-year-old boys.
I wouldn't mind having to look at them straight in the eye, but
having to look up all the time is embarrassing and it hurts my
neck too. When you dance with a girl, they are supposed to be
able to put their hand on your shoulder, not their chin on your
head.

So when Myron asked me at lunch. "Are you going to the
'Getting to Know You' dance?"

I said, "Are you kidding? Nobody's going to that dance."

Myron took a giant bite of his sandwich and said,
"Emrymoday ish gowig."

"Every Monday, what did you say?" I asked.

Myron wiped a large glob of mustard off his chin with his sleeve. "I said, everybody I know is going." Myron looked at the glob of mustard that now decorated his sleeve and without hesitation ground it into his pants. "Everybody, that is, except you."

I stared down at the spot on Myron's pants and then up at a new glob on his chin. At this rate, by the end of lunch, he would be wearing palomino-coloured pants and a white shirt with gold cuffs. "Name one person who's going."

"Me!"

"Besides you."

"Todd Murray."

"Mr Murray, our maths teacher?" Myron nodded. "He has to go. He's the chaperone. Besides, teachers don't count."

"Come on, go." I shook my head no. "For me?" I shook my head no again. "Why not?" This time the mustard had migrated up both cheeks.

"Why do you use so much mustard on your sandwich?" I asked, purposely changing the subject.

"Because I hate the taste of the meat," replied Myron.

"If you hate the taste of the meat so much, why don't you put a different kind of meat on your sandwich?"

"If I put on the meat that I liked, I wouldn't put on any mustard, and I like mustard on my sandwich." I stood up to go. "Not so fast. Why won't you go to the dance? Are you too chicken to go?"

"I don't want to talk about it anymore," I replied. "Finish eating your mustard sandwich and have a good time at the dance. You can tell me about it on Monday."

I thought I had heard the last of it, but after dinner that night my father asked me to go into the den because he wanted to talk to me about something. This usually means I've done something wrong and my mother has delegated my father to handle it.

"I've cleaned up my room," I said. "I did all my homework. I'll read a book for half an hour before I go to sleep, and I took out the trash."

My father smiled. "Why aren't you going to the 'Getting to Know You' dance?"

"How do you know that?" I asked.

"Your mother was talking to Myron's mother and –"

"I don't want to go, that's all. What's the big deal?"

My father lit his pipe and leaned back in his chair. This usually meant he was going to tell me a story about himself when he was my age. "When I was your age and just starting seventh grade like you, my school had a 'Getting to Know You' dance too, and I didn't want to go either. My dad sat me down, just like this, and said to me, 'I'll bet you're a little afraid to go to the dance.' 'Afraid?' I replied. 'I'm not afraid of any school dance.' 'Not of the dance,' he continued, 'but of the girls. Girls can be scary at your age. They act like they feel more comfortable in social situations than boys, but they are just as scared as you are. Go to the dance, act like you know what you're doing, and I'll bet you'll have a good time.' I didn't want to admit it then, but what your grandfather said to me that day made sense and I decided to go to the dance. The night of the dance my father drove me to the school and as I got out of the car he said, 'Break a leg.' That's an expression actors use when they want to wish another actor good luck on the night of a performance. I think he did that purposely because he knew I'd have to be a good actor that night to hide my nervousness. I was nervous that night, but I covered it well and I ended up having a great time. Think about it."

I sat by myself in the den for a long time after Dad left and thought about what he just said. Usually what Dad says is either dumb or old-fashioned. This time he surprised me with something right on. Was he getting smarter?

After I called Myron and told him I had decided to go to the dance I spent half of the next twenty-four hours in and out of the bathroom. It was certainly a local record and probably a national and international one too. I could see myself in the Guinness Book of World Records for Most Trips in One Day to the Bathroom Without Actually Doing Anything.

I hardly ate dinner. After showering I smoothed on a manly

hair gel, splashed on a mentholly after-shave, and sprayed on a musky deodorant, I smelled muskmantholly magnificent. I almost got out of the house with my old sneakers, but my mom made me go back and put on my new slippery loafers.

My father drove Myron and me to the dance. "Break a leg," he yelled as I got out of the car.

"What's that all about?" asked Myron.

"Who knows," I replied. "Probably some weird expression he picked up when he was my age."

When we got to the gym steps, I scuffed the bottom of my new shoes to take away some of the slipperiness. The gym was decorated with blue and white streamers and red, white and yellow balloons. At one end was a large sign picturing a boy and girl dancing. It said "WELCOME, SEVENTH GRADERS". Tables with punch, cookies, pretzels, and potato chips lined both side walls. The bleachers were filled with boys and the dance floor was filled with girls.

Myron and I walked to the top of the bleachers and sat down. I would have been very happy sitting there all evening, but the teacher chaperones had a different agenda. Without any warning they went into the stands and shooed all of the boys out onto the floor. *Time to start acting*, I told myself.

Mr Murray grabbed the microphone and said, "Girls make a circle." When they finished he said, "Boys make a circle around the girl's circle."

"Just what I wanted to do," I said to Myron. "Hold your hand and go around and around in a circle."

"When the music starts," instructed Mr Murray, "I want the girls to circle clockwise and the boys to circle counterclockwise." The music started and around both circles went. "When the music stops I want you to take the person in front of you for a partner."

Things were beginning to get serious. My heart was beating double time to the music and my muskmantholly mist was turning to must. I secretly prayed for the song never to end. My prayer went unanswered and I found myself face to face with a girl – a tall girl – a very tall, muscular girl.

Act calm, I told myself. So what if her grandfather was Paul Bunyan. I smiled, she smiled back. I didn't know what to do next, so I smiled again.

"Introduce yourself to your partner," said Mr Murray.

"I'm Elliot."

"I'm Paula."

Paula Bunyan, I thought. Should I ask if she has a pet ox at home? *Be calm, Elliot. Be calm.*

"To get things warmed up," said Mr Murray, "I thought we might start off with a Mexican hat dance. Cross your hands and take hold of your partner." My palms were soaking wet and I wiped them on my pants before I grabbed Paula's hands. "Left foot, right foot, left-right-left. Do that combination two times. Go." Even though I could tell everyone around me thought this was dumb, we all did it. I could tell my shoes were still a little slippery. "Now, with your hands still crossed, swing your partner around. Go." *Next thing he'll want us to do is a whole dance of this*, I thought. "Now I want you to put both steps together and do them in time to the music."

The music started and Paula jerked me toward her. The one good thing about this kind of dance was that we were still far enough away from each other that I didn't have to talk to her. With a little luck I'd be back in the stands watching in a few minutes.

"Left, right, left-right-left," barked Mr Murray. "Left, right, left-right-left . . . Now swing." Paula started off slowly, but as the music got louder she swung harder. The faster she swung, the dizzier I got. At the apex of the swing either she let go or my sweaty hands slipped away from hers. Either way I found myself spinning and twirling across the floor, straight for the punch bowl. The kids around us stopped to watch this whirling dervish. It seemed as if everyone was staring and pointing.

My left leg hit the table first, full force, causing it to tip forward. The strength of the blow caused my feet to slide out from under me and before I knew it I was on the ground and the table was on top of my legs. My pants were soaked with punch and my shirt was covered with smushed, smashed slivers of pretzels and potato chips.

There was almost complete silence until one of the kids started to laugh. Then everyone laughed. I felt stupid, dumb, and wet. I saw Mr Murray running toward me to help, but Myron arrived first. I brushed myself off. He helped me up. I started to take a step, but my left leg refused to bear any weight and I collapsed in a heap.

The doctor at the hospital showed me the break in the X-ray and told me my leg would be in a full leg cast for at least six weeks.

Since Myron came to the hospital with me, he was the first to sign my cast. He laughed the whole time he was writing. When he finished he said, "Read it."

What he wrote started at my thigh and went down the entire length of the cast. It said, "Remember what your dad said to you when you got out of the car? I know you're supposed to listen to your parents, but this is ridiculous." I looked up at Myron, who was still smiling. "Your cast will be off just in time for the Thanksgiving Dance. Going?"

UNCLE TREVOR'S
MAGIC FLYING SLIPPERS

IAN McMILLAN

MY UNCLE TREVOR'S DAFT. Daft as a carrot, my mother always says. "Uncle Trevor: daft as a carrot," she'll say when she sees him on the street. He doesn't care. He'll just wave and smile.

Because my Uncle Trevor's daft, nobody ever believes him. He once ran into our house in a raincoat and a big hat and shouted, "Look out, everybody, the dam's burst! Run for your lives! Get to the high ground as fast as you can!" Then he ran out of the house again. My younger sister Bethany believed him and started to cry, until my mother pointed out there was no dam within a hundred miles of our house and we were in no danger. Uncle Trevor was in danger, though. He was in danger of my mother giving him a smack round the head for making Bethany cry.

When my mother caught up with him he was outside in the garden, shaking with laughter. My mother said, "It's just not funny, Trev!" But he wouldn't stop laughing, and eventually my mother had to laugh as well. That's the thing about Uncle Trevor: he's so daft he just makes you laugh, unless you're our Bethany. My mother still gave him a smack round the head, but it didn't stop him laughing.

Well, maybe for a second.

The thing is, I'm not sure that Uncle Trevor really is that daft. I remember the time he told us he'd found a gold ring at the bottom of his garden. Nobody believed him, but then he took it to the museum in town and they said it was really old and valuable. Uncle Trevor appeared on the local TV news and got his picture in the paper. He said he'd known it was a valuable ring because he'd worked in a jeweller's shop when he was young. I didn't know whether to believe him or not. Bit of a mystery man, Uncle Trevor.

So when Uncle Trevor came round to our house and announced that he'd made some magic flying slippers, nobody believed him.

"It's true!" he said, his voice rising and almost shattering into a thousand bits like it did when he got excited. He said he was launching the magic flying slippers the next day at twelve o'clock at the back of his house, and we were all welcome to come.

"How did you make them?" I asked.

He smiled. "I used *secret* ingredients. But I can let you know that there's wood involved, hard wood, and more paper clips than you've ever seen. There's water, too. Cold water."

"How do they fly?" I asked.

He shook his head. "I can't tell you that," he said. "But there's no engine. No engine at all."

My mother just turned back to her book, but I said I'd go. I didn't really know what to think about magic flying slippers. Obviously they weren't really magic and they weren't going to fly. But then, it *was* Uncle Trevor.

In the end I was the only person to turn up, but Uncle Trevor didn't seem too disappointed. He had one last look to see if anyone else was coming, then he shook his head.

He took me down to the bottom of his garden and told me to stand behind the shed.

"Why do I have to stand here?" I asked.

"Because you'll get a better view!" he replied, his voice crinkling round the edges.

I stood at the back of the shed for ages, counting the nails that were holding it together. Finally, Uncle Trevor shouted, "Right, I'm just going to do 'The Flying Slipper Rap', and then you'll see the slippers fly!"

There was a pause of about ten seconds, and then I heard what I thought were pebbles landing on the shed roof. Until I realized it was Uncle Trevor snapping his fingers. Finally the rap began. Uncle Trevor might be good at finding valuable rings, but he wasn't much good at rapping. He was trying to sound cool, and it was a disaster:

> "Flying slippers
> You're gonna fly
> Up in the sky
> Way up high!
>
> Flying slippers
> In the air
> Gonna end up
> Don't know where!
>
> Flying slippers
> Up to the stars
> Landing in a crater
> Far side of Mars!"

Then there was a little bang that sounded like a balloon popping, and a puff of purple smoke, and the slippers flew over the shed – and I caught them, one in each hand. (It wasn't hard. They were flying really slowly.) I looked at them. They looked like perfectly ordinary slippers. The kind your granddad might wear.

It was amazing, really. I hadn't actually believed they were going to fly, but there they were, in my hands, and there they'd been, flying through the air like a couple of birds. Red and blue checked birds, with thermal lining.

Uncle Trevor came round from the other side of the shed.

170

He took the slippers from me. "What do you reckon?" he said. "Flying slippers, or what?"

"How do they fly?" I asked.

Uncle Trevor tapped the side of his nose. "That's a secret, I'm afraid. I had to promise The Dood not to tell anybody."

"Who's 'The Dood'?"

"The guy who came round to my house the other night and asked if I wanted to know how to make flying slippers!"

"What did he look like?"

"He looked like a dude," said Uncle Trevor. "A real dude."

At home that night I told my mother about Uncle Trevor's magic flying slippers.

My mother laughed. "It's another one of Trevor's stories," she said.

"But I saw them fly over the shed," I protested. "And I caught them!"

"Yes, but did you see *how* they flew?" my mother asked.

I shook my head.

"You go to Trevor's tomorrow and ask if you can see them setting off, actually starting to fly. I think you'll find he's just throwing them. Don't forget – he's as daft as a carrot!"

Well, that's what I'd do. I'd go and see how they flew. My mother was the daft one. She was dafter than a carrot. She was as daft as a turnip!

The next day I went to Uncle Trevor's and asked if I could see the slippers fly.

"No problem!" he said. "Just go behind the shed and watch the skies. I'll be out in a minute."

"No, I want to see them actually take off," I said. "I want to see how you do it."

Uncle Trevor looked really sad. "I'd like to show you, lad, but I'm afraid I can't. You see, The Dood said that only I could be part of the mystery of why and how the slippers fly. Sorry! I'd like to help, but . . ."

I felt really cross. I wanted to cry.

171

"My mother was right about the slippers!" I shouted. "They're not magic at all! I bet you're just throwing them! It's just another one of your stories!"

Uncle Trevor looked shocked.

"OK then, I'll have a word with The Dood tonight," he said. "He's coming round later with some *Flying Slipper Monthlies*. I'll tell him you're a good man, and you can keep a secret. I can't promise anything, but come round tomorrow and we'll see."

The next day I went to Uncle Trevor's. He was watching for me through the window. There was a thin man in a huge woolly hat standing beside him. The thin man looked at me and pointed. Uncle Trevor nodded. The thin man beckoned me into the house.

Uncle Trevor and the thin man stood looking at me.

"This is Norman the Dood," Uncle Trevor said. "Shake hands."

The Dood stretched out his green hand and I shook it. It was cool and dry. He twisted his hand and twisted it again. He let go of my hand, then grabbed it again. He let go again, snapped his fingers, put his thumb up, slapped my hand, got hold of it and shook it again. It was the worst impression of a cool handshake I'd ever seen.

Then he started to rap:

> *"Is this the kid?*
> *Is this the feller?*
> *His hair is brown*
> *But his teeth are yeller!"*

he said. The Dood was also a terrible rapper, worse than Uncle Trevor, if that was possible. His rapping was as bad as his handshake.

"That's him," said Uncle Trevor to The Dood. "What do you think?"

> *"He looks like the kinda kid*
> *We can trust*

Feels like he's been showered
With trusting dust
So I think that we can trust him, Trevor;
He's got a lovely smile but he don't look clever!"

Not only was he the worst rapper in the world, and the most insulting, he was also the loudest. Uncle Trevor's neighbour started knocking on the wall.

"Can you keep the noise down a bit?" said Uncle Trevor.

"Not when *The Vibe* is on me!" yelled Norman the Dood.

The neighbour knocked on the wall again, and Norman used the rhythm of the knocking to start his next feeble rhyme:

"Flying slippers
Day trippers
Star jumpers
Sky divers
Moving through the air
From here to there
Feel the wind
Catch in your hair
From A to B
From X to Zee
You can see
The top of a tree
When you're flying free
Oh yes, when you're flying free!"

The neighbour seemed to work out that the knocking was helping the rapping, so he stopped and Norman the Dood's rap ground to a halt, like a train slowing down at a broken signal.

Uncle Trevor looked at me. "I think he's saying, in his own way, that he wants you to pilot the slippers," he said.

Norman slapped me hard on the back, which I took to mean "yes".

I was torn. Me, pilot the slippers? I could only just pilot a pair of skates! I got lost walking upstairs! I wasn't sure if I should;

173

then again, I wasn't sure if they even worked. Then again, I wasn't sure if I wanted them to work. Then again, I'd never know if they worked if I didn't try. Then again . . . There wasn't another "Then again". I'd have to put on the slippers and fly.

So there I was, standing on the lawn in the magic flying slippers. Uncle Trevor was doing his rap, and Norman the Dood was standing with his mouth open, looking up. Uncle Trevor had explained that he imagined the slippers in the sky, and that helped them to take off. I wasn't sure if I believed him. But I soon did.

The slippers started to tremble. Then they started to shake. Then they started to hover. Then they popped and purple smoke came out of them. Then they started to fly.

It's a funny thing when the slippers you're wearing start to take off. It's not like taking off in a plane. It's like getting taller very quickly or going up in a glass lift or slowly opening the curtains in a hotel room and finding you're on the top floor. I went upwards, and then I went forwards. You have to sort of run to keep your balance, and that's hard at first, but after a while you get used to it, and then it's great. I started by flying round the garden, waving to Uncle Trevor and Norman. Then I flew down the street. Then I flew over the town, and my legs never got tired, never got tired at all.

I've never stopped flying since, and it's fantastic. I swoop down like a bird and grab sandwiches from people's hands as they sit having a picnic. I fly over the sea for days at a time, and it's like flying over a map, a dancing map. I fly as high up as I can and the air is thin but it's so clean it feels like I'm having a bath in the pale sky that's nearly in space.

If you look up now, and you think you see a plane in the distance, it'll be me. If you see what looks like a big bird landing in the trees, it'll be me. And if you hear a whooshing sound past your house late at night, you know who it'll be. And I do miss my mum and Bethany sometimes, but every now and then I fly over the garden and wave, and I'm sure they know it's me, even though I'm really high up.

So never forget. Carrots aren't daft. They're clever. Just like my Uncle Trevor and his mate Norman the Dood.

Go out now. Put this book down, and look up in the sky. You'll see me. Me and my magic flying slippers.

BLABBER MOUTH

MORRIS GLEITZMAN

It's Rowena Batts' first day at her new school and things aren't going well. Anyone would be nervous, and Rowena has an added problem – she is unable to speak. But Rowena can look after herself, as the aggravating Darryn Peck is about to find out.

I'M SO DUMB.

I never thought I'd say that about myself, but after what I've just done I deserve it.

How could have I have messed up my first day here so totally and completely?

Two hours ago, when I walked into this school for the first time, the sun was shining, the birds were singing and, apart from a knot in my guts the size of Tasmania, life was great.

Now here I am, locked in the stationery cupboard.

Just me, a pile of exam papers and what smells like one of last year's cheese and devon sandwiches.

Cheer up exam papers, cheer up ancient sanger, if you think you're unpopular, take a look at me.

I wish those teachers would stop shouting at me to unlock the door and come out. I don't want to come out. I want to sit here in the dark with my friend the sandwich.

Oh no, now Ms Dunning's trying to pick the lock with the

staff-room knife. One of the other teachers is telling her not to cut herself. The principal's telling her not to damage the staff-room knife.

I hope she doesn't cut herself because she was really good to me this morning.

I was an Orange-to-Dubbo-phone-line-in-a-heap-sized bundle of nerves when I walked into that classroom this morning with everyone staring. Even though we've been in the district over a week, and I've seen several of the kids in the main street, they still stared.

I didn't blame them. In small country towns you don't get much to stare at. Just newcomers and old men who dribble, mostly.

Ms Dunning was great. She told everyone to remember their manners or she'd kick them in the bum, and everyone laughed. Then when she saw the letters me and Dad had photocopied she said it was the best idea she'd seen since microwave pizza, and gave me permission to hand them round.

I watched anxiously while all the kids read the letter. I was pretty pleased with it, but you can never tell how an audience is going to react.

"G'day," the letter said, "my name's Rowena Batts and, as you've probably noticed by now, I can't speak. Don't worry, but, we can still be friends 'cause I can write, draw, point, nod, shake my head, screw up my nose and do sign language. I used to go to a special school but the government closed it down. The reason I can't speak is I was born with some bits missing from my throat. (It's OK, I don't leak.) Apart from that, I'm completely normal and my hobbies are reading, watching TV and driving my Dad's tractor. I hope we can be friends, yours sincerely, Rowena Batts."

That letter took me about two hours to write last night, not counting the time I spent arguing with Dad about the spelling, so I was pleased that most people read it all the way through.

Some kids smiled.

Some laughed, but in a nice way.

A few nudged each other and gave me smirky looks.

178

"OK," said Ms Dunning, "let's all say g'day to Rowena."

"G'day," everyone chorused, which I thought was a bit humiliating for them, but Ms Dunning meant well.

I gave them the biggest grin I could, even though Tasmania was trying to crawl up my throat.

A couple of the kids didn't say g'day, they just kept on with the smirky looks.

One of them was a boy with red lips and ginger hair and there was something about his extra-big smirk that made me think even then that I was probably going to have trouble with him.

"Right," said Ms Dunning after she'd sat me down next to a girl with white hair who was still only halfway through my letter, "who's on frogs today?" She looked at a chart on the wall next to a tank with some small green frogs in it.

"Darryn Peck," she said.

The kid with the big red smirk got up and swaggered over to the tank.

"Clean it thoroughly," warned Ms Dunning, "or I'll feed you to them."

We all laughed and Darryn Peck gave her a rude sign behind her back. A couple of kids laughed again and Ms Dunning was just about to turn back to Darryn when a woman came to the door and said there was a phone call for her in the office.

"Ignore the floor show," Ms Dunning told us, giving Darryn Peck a long look, "and read something interesting. I'll only be a sec."

As soon as she'd gone, Darryn Peck started.

"I can speak sign language," he said loudly, smirking right at me. Then he gave me the same finger he'd given Ms Dunning.

About half the class laughed.

I decided to ignore him.

The girl next to me was still having trouble with my letter. She had her ruler under the word "sincerely" and was frowning at it.

I found my pen, leaned over, crossed out "Yours sincerely" and wrote "No bull". She looked at it for a moment, then grinned at me.

"Rowena Batts," said Darryn Peck. "What sort of a name is Batts?" Do you fly around at night and suck people's blood?"

Hardly anyone laughed and I didn't blame them. I've had better insults from kids with permanent brain damage.

I thought about asking him what kind of a name Peck was, and did he get sore knees from eating with the chooks, but then I remembered nobody there would be able to understand my hand movements, and the trouble with writing insults is it takes years.

"My parents'd go for a kid like you," said Darryn, even louder. "They're always saying they wish I'd lose my voice."

Nobody laughed.

Darryn could see he was losing his audience.

Why didn't I treat that as a victory and ignore him and swap addresses with the slow reader next to me?

Because I'm not just mute, I'm dumb.

"Your parents must be really pleased you're a freak," brayed Darryn. "Or are they freaks too and haven't noticed?"

He shouldn't have said that.

Dad can look after himself, but Mum died when I was born and if anyone says anything bad about her I get really angry.

I got really angry.

Tasmania sprouted volcanoes and the inside of my head filled up with molten lava.

I leapt across the room and snatched the frog Darryn Peck was holding and squeezed his cheeks hard so his red lips popped open and stuffed the frog into his mouth and grabbed the sticky tape from the art table and wound it round and round his head till there was none left.

The others all stared at me, mouths open, horrified. Then they quickly closed their mouths.

I stood there while the lava cooled in my head and Darryn Peck gurgled and the other kids backed away.

Then I realised what I'd done.

Lost all my friends before I'd even made them.

I ran out of the room and down the corridor past a startled Ms Dunning and just as she was calling out I saw a cupboard door with a key in it and threw myself in and locked it.

The smell in here's getting worse.

I don't think it's a cheese and devon sandwich after all, I think it's a dead frog.

I'm not opening the door.

I just want to sit here in the dark and pretend I'm at my old school with my old friends.

It's not easy because the teachers out there in the corridor are making such a racket scurrying around and muttering to each other and yelling at kids to get back in the classroom.

Ms Dunning's just been to phone Dad, and the principal's just asked if anyone's got a crowbar in their car.

It doesn't sound as though anyone has, or if they have, they don't want to go and get it.

I don't blame them. Who'd want to walk all the way to the staff car park for the least popular girl in the school?

Dad arrived just in time.

I was getting desperate because the smell was making me feel sick and Ms Dunning pleading with me through the door was making me feel guilty and the sound of an electric drill being tested was making me feel scared.

But I couldn't bring myself to open the door and face all those horrified kids.

And angry teachers.

And Mr. Fowler the principal, who'd skinned his knuckles trying to force the lock with a stapler.

Not by myself.

Then I heard a truck pull up outside.

I've never been so pleased to hear a vibrating tailgate. The tailgate on our truck has vibrated ever since Dad took the old engine out and put in a turbo-powered one with twin exhausts.

There were more scurrying sounds from out in the corridor and then Ms Dunning called through the door.

"Rowena, your father's here. If you come out now we'll try and keep him calm."

I grinned to myself in the dark. She obviously didn't know my father.

181

I took a deep breath and opened the door.

The corridor was full of faces, all staring at me.

The principal, looking grim and holding a bandaged hand.

Ms Dunning, looking concerned.

The other teachers, looking annoyed.

Kids peeking out of classrooms, some horrified, some smirking.

Plus a couple of blokes in bushfire brigade overalls carrying a huge electric drill, and a man in a dustcoat with *Vic's Hardware* embroidered on the pocket holding a big bunch of keys, and an elderly woman in a yellow oilskin jacket with *State Emergency Service* printed on it.

All staring at me.

I don't think anybody said anything. But I wouldn't have heard them if they had because my heart was pounding in my ears like a stump excavator.

Then the door at the other end of the corridor swung open with a bang and all the heads turned.

It was Dad.

As he walked slowly down the corridor, taking in the situation, everyone stared at him even harder than they'd stared at me.

I didn't blame them. People usually stare at Dad the first time they see him. They're not being rude, it's just that most people have never seen an apple farmer wearing goanna-skin boots, black jeans, a studded belt with a polished metal cow's skull buckle, a black shirt with white tassels and a black cowboy hat.

Dad came up to me, looking concerned.

"You OK, Tonto?" he asked.

He always calls me Tonto. I think it's a character from a TV show he used to watch when he was a kid. I'd be embarrassed if he said it out loud, but it's OK when he says it with his hands because nobody else can understand. Dad always talks to me with his hands. He reckons two people can have a better conversation when they're both speaking the same language.

"I'm fine, Dad," I replied.

Everyone was staring at our hands, wondering what we were saying.

"Tough day, huh?" said Dad.

"Fairly tough," I said.

Dad gave me a sympathetic smile, then turned and met the gaze of all the people in the corridor.

Mr Fowler, the principal, stepped forward.

"We can't have a repeat of this sort of thing, Mr Batts," he said.

"It was just first day nerves," said Ms Dunning. "I'm sure it won't happen again."

Dad cleared his throat.

My stomach sank.

When Dad clears his throat it usually means one thing.

It did today.

He moved slowly around the semicircle of people, looking each of them in the eye, and sang to them.

Their mouths fell open.

Mr Fowler stepped back.

The hardware bloke dropped his keys.

As usual, Dad sang a country and western number from his record collection. He's got this huge collection of records by people with names like Slim Dusty and Carla Tamworth – the big black plastic records you play on one of those old-fashioned record players with a needle.

This one was about lips like a graveyard and a heart like a fairground and I knew Dad was singing about me.

Part of me felt proud and grateful.

The other part of me wanted to creep back into the cupboard and shut the door.

Several of the teachers looked as though they wanted to as well.

Dad thinks country and western is the best music ever written and he assumes everyone else does too. They usually don't, mostly because he doesn't get many of the notes right.

When he'd finished, and the hardware bloke had picked up his keys, Dad put an arm round my shoulders.

"Ladies and gentleman," he announced, "Rowena Batts is

taking the rest of the day off. Apologies for the inconvenience, and if anyone's out of pocket, give us a hoy and I'll bung you a bag of apples."

He steered me down the corridor.

Just before we went out the door, I glanced back. Nobody had moved. Everyone looked stunned, except Ms Dunning, who had a big grin on her face.

In the truck driving into town, I told Dad what had happened. He hardly took his eyes off my hands the whole time except when he had to swerve to avoid the war memorial. When I told him about the frog in Darryn Peck's mouth he laughed so much his hat fell off.

I didn't think any of it was funny.

What's funny about everyone thinking you're a psychopath who's cruel to frogs and not wanting to touch you with a bargepole?

Just thinking about it made my eyes hot and prickly.

Dad saw this and stopped laughing.

"OK, Tonto," he said, steering with his knees, "let's go and rot our teeth."

We went and had chocolate milkshakes with marshmallows floating on top, and Dad did such a good imitation of Darryn Peck with the frog in his mouth that I couldn't help laughing.

Especially when the man in the milk bar thought Dad was choking on a marshmallow.

Then we played Intergalactic Ice Invaders and I was twenty-seven thousand points ahead when the milk bar man asked us to leave because Dad was making too much noise. I guess the milk bar man must have been right because as we left, a man in a brown suit glared at us from the menswear shop next door.

We went to the pub and had lemon squash and played pool. Dad slaughtered me as usual, but I didn't mind. One of the things I really like about Dad is he doesn't fake stuff just to make you feel better. So when he says good things you know he means it. Like on the pool table today when I cracked a backspin for the first time and he said how proud it made him because he hadn't done it till he was thirteen.

When we got back here the sun was going down but Dad let me drive the tractor round the orchard a few times while he stood up on the engine cover waving a branch to keep the mozzies off us.

I was feeling so good by then I didn't even mind his singing.

We came inside and made fried eggs and apple fritters, which everyone thinks sounds yukky but that's only because they don't know how to make it. You've got to leave the eggs runny.

After dinner we watched telly, then I went to bed.

"If you ever get really depressed about anything," I said, "feel free to use the school stationery cupboard, but take a peg for your nose."

Dad grinned.

"Thanks, Tonto," he said. "Anyone who doesn't want to be your mate has got bubbles in the brain. Or frogs in the mouth."

I hugged him again and thought how lucky I am to have such a great dad.

HOW TOM BEAT
CAPTAIN NAJORK AND
HIS HIRED SPORTSMEN

RUSSELL HOBAN

TOM LIVED WITH HIS MAIDEN AUNT, Miss Fidget Wonkham-Strong. She wore an iron hat, and took no nonsense from anyone. Where she walked the flowers drooped, and when she sang the trees all shivered.

Tom liked to fool around. He fooled around with sticks and stones and crumpled paper, with mewses and passages and dustbins, with bent nails and broken glass and holes in fences.

He fooled around with mud, and stomped and squelched and slithered through it.

He fooled around on high-up things that shook and wobbled and teetered.

He fooled around with dropping things from bridges into rivers and fishing them out.

He fooled around with barrels in alleys.

When Aunt Fidget Wonkham-Strong asked him what he was doing, Tom said that he was fooling around.

"It looks very like playing to me," said Aunt Fidget Wonkham-Strong. "Too much playing is not good, and you play too much. You had better stop it and do something useful."

"All right," said Tom.

But he did not stop. He did a little fooling around with two or three cigar bands and a paper clip.

At dinner Aunt Fidget Wonkham-Strong, wearing her iron hat, said, "Eat your mutton and your cabbage-and-potato sog."

"All right," said Tom. He ate it.

After dinner Aunt Fidget Wonkham-Strong said, "Now learn off pages 65 to 76 of the Nautical Almanac, and that will teach you not to fool around so much."

"All right," said Tom.

He learned them off.

"From now on I shall keep an eye on you," Aunt Fidget Wonkham-Strong said, "and if you do not stop fooling around I shall send for Captain Najork and his hired sportsmen."

"Who is Captain Najork?" said Tom.

"Captain Najork," said Aunt Fidget Wonkham-Strong, "is seven feet tall, with eyes like fire, a voice like thunder, and a handlebar moustache. His trousers are always freshly pressed, his blazer is immaculate, his shoes are polished mirror-bright, and he is every inch a terror. When Captain Najork is sent for he comes up the river in his pedal boat, with his hired sportsmen pedalling hard. He teaches fooling-around boys the lesson they so badly need, and it is not one that they soon forget."

Aunt Fidget Wonkham-Strong kept an eye on Tom. He did not stop fooling around. He did low and muddy fooling around and he did high and wobbly fooling around. He fooled around with dropping things off bridges and he fooled around with barrels in alleys.

"Very well," said Aunt Fidget Wonkham-Strong at table in her iron hat. "Eat your greasy bloaters."

Tom ate them.

"I have warned you," said Aunt Fidget Wonkham-Strong, "that I should send for Captain Najork if you did not stop fooling around. I have done that. As you like to play so much, you shall play against Captain Najork and his hired sportsmen. They play hard games and they play them jolly hard. Prepare yourself."

"All right," said Tom. He fooled around with a bottle-top and a burnt match.

The next day Captain Najork came up the river with his hired sportsmen pedalling his pedal boat.

They came ashore smartly, carrying an immense brown-paper parcel. They marched into the garden, one, two, three, four. Captain Najork was only six feet tall. His eyes were not like fire, his voice was not like thunder.

"Right," said Captain Najork. "Where is the sportive infant?"

"There," said Aunt Fidget Wonkham-Strong.

"Here," said Tom.

"Right," said the Captain. "We shall play womble, muck, and sneedball, in that order." The hired sportsmen sniggered as they undid the immense brown-paper parcel, set up the womble run, the ladders and the net, and distributed the rakes and stakes.

"How do you play womble?" said Tom.

"You'll find out," said Captain Najork.

"Who's on my side?" said Tom.

"Nobody," said Captain Najork. "Let's get started."

Womble turned out to be a shaky, high-up, wobbling and teetering sort of a game, and Tom was used to that kind of fooling around. The Captain's side raked first. Tom staked. The hired sportsmen played so hard that they wombled too fast, and were shaky with the rakes. Tom fooled around the way he always did, and all his stakes dropped true. When it was his turn to rake he did not let Captain Najork and the hired sportsmen score a single rung, and at the end of the snetch he won by six ladders.

"Right," said Caption Najork, clenching his teeth. "Muck next. Same sides."

The court was laid out at low tide in the river mud. Tom mucked first, and slithered through the marks while the hired sportsmen poled and shovelled. Tom had fooled around with mud so much that he scored time after time.

Captain Najork's men poled too hard and shovelled too fast and tired themselves out. Tom just mucked about and fooled around, and when the tide came in he led the opposition 673 to 49.

"Really," said Aunt Fidget Wonkham-Strong to Captain Najork, "you must make an effort to teach this boy a lesson."

"Some boys learn hard," said the Captain, chewing his moustache. "Now for sneedball."

The hired sportsmen brought out the ramp, the slide, the barrel, the bobble, the sneeding tongs, the bar, and the grapples. Tom saw at once that sneedball was like several kinds of fooling around that he was particularly good at. Partly it was like dropping things off bridges into rivers and fishing them out and partly it was like fooling around with barrels in alleys.

"I had better tell you," said the Captain to Tom, "that I played in the Sneedball Finals five years running."

"They couldn't have been very final if you had to keep doing it for five years," said Tom. He motioned the Captain aside, away from Aunt Fidget Wonkham-Strong. "Let's make this interesting," he said.

"What do you mean?" said the Captain.

"Let's play *for* something," said Tom. "Let's say if I win I get your pedal boat."

"What do I get if *I* win?" said the Captain. "Because I am certainly going to win *this* one."

"You can have Aunt Fidget Wonkham-Strong," said Tom.

"She's impressive," said the Captain. "I admit that freely. A very impressive lady."

"She fancies you," said Tom. "I can tell by the way she looks sideways at you from underneath her iron hat."

"No!" said the Captain.

"Yes," said Tom.

"And you'll part with her if she'll have me?" said the Captain.

"It's the only sporting thing to do," said Tom.

"Agreed then!" said the Captain. "By George! I'm almost sorry that I'm going to have to teach you a lesson by beating you at sneedball."

"Let's get started," said Tom.

The hired sportsmen had first slide. Captain Najork himself barrelled, and he and his men played like demons. But Tom tonged the bobble in the same fooling-around way that he fished things out of rivers, and he quickly moved into the lead. Captain Najork sweated big drops, and he slid his barrel too hard so it hit the stop and slopped over. But Tom just fooled around, and when it was his slide he never spilled a drop.

Darkness fell, but they shot up flares and went on playing. By three o'clock in the morning Tom had won by 85 to 10. As the last flare went up above the garden he looked down from the ramp at the defeated Captain and his hired sportsmen and he said, "Maybe that will teach you not to fool around with a boy who knows how to fool around."

Captain Najork broke down and wept, but Aunt Fidget Wonkham-Strong had him put to bed and brought him peppermint tea, and then he felt better.

Tom took his boat and pedalled to the next town down the river. There he advertised in the newspaper for a new aunt. When he found one that he liked, he told her, "No greasy bloaters, no mutton and no cabbage-and-potato sog. No Nautical Almanac. And I do lots of fooling around. Those are my conditions."

The new aunt's name was Bundlejoy Cosysweet. She had a floppy hat with flowers on it. She had long, long hair.

"That sounds fine to me," she said. "We'll have a go."

Aunt Fidget Wonkham-Strong married Captain Najork even though he had lost the sneedball game, and they were very happy together. She made the hired sportsmen learn off pages of the Nautical Almanac every night after dinner.

THE HITCHHIKER

ROALD DAHL

I HAD A NEW CAR. It was an exciting toy, a big BMW 3.3 Li, which means 3.3 litre, long wheelbase, fuel injection. It had a top speed of 129 mph and terrific acceleration. The body was pale blue. The seats inside were darker blue and they were made of leather, genuine soft leather of the finest quality. The windows were electrically operated and so was the sunroof. The radio aerial popped up when I switched on the radio, and disappeared when I switched it off. The powerful engine growled and grunted impatiently at slow speeds, but at sixty miles an hour the growling stopped and the motor began to purr with pleasure.

I was driving up to London by myself. It was a lovely June day. They were haymaking in the fields and there were buttercups along both sides of the road. I was whispering along at 70 mph, leaning back comfortably in my seat, with no more than a couple of fingers resting lightly on the wheel to keep her steady. Ahead of me I saw a man thumbing a lift. I touched the brake and brought the car to a stop beside him. I always stopped for hitchhikers. I knew just how it used to feel to be standing on the side of a country road watching the cars go by. I hated the drivers for pretending they didn't see me, especially the ones in big empty cars with three empty seats. The large expensive cars seldom stopped. It was always the smaller ones that offered you a lift, or the rusty ones or the ones that were already crammed full of children and the driver would say, "I think we can squeeze in one more."

The hitchhiker poked his head through the open window and said, "Going to London, guv'nor?"

"Yes," I said. "Jump in."

He got in and I drove on.

He was a small ratty-faced man with grey teeth. His eyes were dark and quick and clever, like rat's eyes, and his ears were slightly pointed at the top. He had a cloth cap on his head and he was wearing a greyish-coloured jacket with enormous pockets. The grey jacket, together with the quick eyes and the pointed ears, made him look more than anything like some sort of huge human rat.

"What part of London are you headed for?" I asked him.

"I'm going right through London and out the other side," he said. "I'm goin' to Epsom, for the races. It's Derby Day today."

"So it is," I said. "I wish I were going with you. I love betting on horses."

"I never bet on horses," he said. "I don't even watch 'em run. That's a stupid silly business."

"Then why do you go?" I asked.

He didn't seem to like that question. His ratty little face went absolutely blank and he sat there staring straight ahead at the road, saying nothing.

"I expect you help to work the betting machines or something like that, " I said.

"That's even sillier," he answered. "There's no fun working them lousy machines and selling tickets to mugs. Any fool could do that."

There was a long silence. I decided not to question him any more. I remembered how irritated I used to get in my hitchhiking days when drivers kept asking *me* questions. Where are you going? Why are you going there? What's your job? Are you married? Do you have a girlfriend? What's her name? How old are you? And so forth and so forth. I used to hate it.

"I'm sorry," I said. "It's none of my business what you do. The trouble is I'm a writer, and most writers are terribly nosy."

"You write books?" he asked.

"Yes."

"Writin' books is OK," he said. "It's what I call a skilled trade. I'm in a skilled trade too. The folks I despise is them that spend all their lives doin' crummy old routine jobs with no skill in 'em at all. You see what I mean?"

"Yes."

"The secret of life," he said, "is to become very very good at somethin' that's very very 'ard to do."

"Like you," I said.

"Exactly. You and me both."

"What makes you think that *I'm* any good at my job?" I asked. "There's an awful lot of bad writers around."

"You wouldn't be driving about in a car like this if you weren't no good at it," he answered. "It must've cost a tidy packet, this little job."

"It wasn't cheap."

"What can she do flat out?" he asked.

"One hundred and twenty-nine miles an hour," I told him.

"I'll bet she won't do it."

"I'll bet she will."

"All car-makers is liars," he said. "You can buy any car you like and it'll never do what the makers say it will in the ads."

"This one will."

"Open 'er up then and prove it," he said. "Go on guv'nor, open 'er up and let's see what she'll do."

There is a traffic circle at Chalfont St Peter and immediately beyond there's a long straight section of divided highway. We came out of the circle onto the highway and I pressed my foot hard down on the accelerator. The big car leaped forward as though she'd been stung. In ten seconds or so, we were doing ninety.

"Lovely!" he cried. "Beautiful! Keep goin'!"

I had the accelerator jammed down against the floor and I held it there.

"One hundred!" he shouted. "A hundred and five! A hundred and ten! A hundred and fifteen! Go on! Don't slack off!"

I was in the outside lane and we flashed past several cars as though they were standing still – a green Mini, a big cream-coloured Citroen, a white Land Rover, a huge truck with a container on the back, an orange-coloured Volkswagen Minibus . . .

"A hundred and twenty!" my passenger shouted, jumping up and down. "Go on! Go on! Get 'er up to one-two-nine!"

At that moment, I heard the scream of a police siren. It was so loud it seemed to be right inside the car, and then a cop on a motorcycle loomed up alongside us in the inside lane and went past us and raised a hand for us to stop.

"Oh, my sainted aunt!" I said. "That's torn it!"

The cop must have doing about a hundred and thirty when he passed us, and he took plenty of time slowing down. Finally, he pulled to the side of the road and I pulled in beside him. "I didn't know police motorcycles could *go* as fast as that," I said rather lamely.

"That one can," my passenger said. "It's the same make as yours. It's a BMW R90S. Fastest bike on the road. That's what they're usin' nowadays."

The cop got off his motorcycle and leaned the machine sideways onto its prop stand. Then he took off his gloves and placed them carefully on the seat. He was in no hurry now. He had us where he wanted us and he knew it.

"This is real trouble," I said. "I don't like it one little bit."

"Don't talk to 'im more than necessary, you understand," my companion said. "Just sit tight and keep mum."

Like an executioner approaching his victim, the cop came strolling slowly towards us. He was a big meaty man with a belly, and his blue breeches were skin-tight around enormous thighs. His goggles were pulled up onto the helmet, showing a smouldering red face with wide cheeks.

We sat there like guilty schoolboys, waiting for him to arrive.

"Watch out for this man," my passenger whispered, "'e looks mean as the devil."

The cop came round to my open window and placed one meaty hand on the sill. "What's the hurry?" he said.

"No hurry, officer," I answered.

"Perhaps there's a woman in the back having a baby and you're rushing her to hospital? Is that it?"

"No, officer."

"Or perhaps your house is on fire and you're dashing home to rescue the family from upstairs?" His voice was dangerously soft and mocking.

"My house isn't on fire, officer."

"In that case," he said, "you've got yourself into a nasty mess, haven't you? Do you know what the speed limit is in this country?"

"Seventy," I said.

"And do you mind telling me exactly what speed you were doing just now?"

I shrugged and didn't say anything.

When he spoke next, he raised his voice so loud that I jumped. *"One hundred and twenty miles per hour!"* he barked. "That's *fifty* miles an hour over the limit."

He turned his head and spat out a big gob of spit. It landed on the wing of my car and started sliding down over my beautiful blue paint. Then he turned back again and stared hard at my passenger. "And who are you?" he asked sharply.

"He's a hitchhiker," I said. "I'm giving him a lift."

"I didn't ask you," he said. "I asked him."

"'Ave I done somethin' wrong?" my passenger asked. His voice was soft and oily as haircream.

"That's more than likely," the cop answered. "Anyway, you're a witness. I'll deal with you in a minute. Driver's licence," he snapped, holding out his hand.

I gave him my driver's licence.

He unbuttoned the left-hand breast pocket of his tunic and brought out the dreaded book of tickets. Carefully he copied the name and address from my licence. Then he gave it back to me. He strolled around to the front of the car and read the number from the licence plate and wrote that down as well. He filled in the date, the time and the details of my offence. Then he tore out the top copy of the ticket. But before handing it to me, he checked that all the information had come through clearly on his own carbon copy. Finally, he replaced the book in his breast pocket and fastened the button.

"Now you," he said to my passenger, and he walked around to the other side of the car. From the other breast pocket he produced a small black notebook. "Name?" he snapped.

"Michael Fish," my passenger said.

"Address?"

"Fourteen, Windsor Lane, Luton."

"Show me something to prove this is your real name and address," the policeman said.

My passenger fished in his pockets and came out with a driver's licence of his own. The policeman checked the name and address and handed it back to him. "What's your job?" he asked sharply.

"I'm an 'od carrier."

"A *what?*"

"An 'od carrier."

"Spell it."

"H-o-d c-a –"

"That'll do. And what's a hod carrier, may I ask?"

"An 'od carrier, officer, is a person 'oo carries the cement up the ladder to the bricklayer. And the 'od is what 'ee carries it in. It's got a long 'andle, and on the top you've got bits of wood set at an angle . . ."

"All right, all right. Who's your employer?"

"Don't 'ave one. I'm unemployed."

The cop wrote this down in the black notebook. Then he returned the book to his pocket and did up the button.

"When I get back to the station I'm going to do a little checking up on you," he said to my passenger.

"Me? What've I done wrong?" the rat-faced man asked.

"I don't like your face, that's all," the cop said. "And we just might have a picture of it somewhere in our files." He strolled round the car and returned to my window.

"I suppose you know you're in serious trouble," he said to me.

"Yes, officer."

"You won't be driving this fancy car of yours for a very long time, not after *we've* finished with you. You won't be driving *any* car again, come to that, for several years. And a good thing, too. I hope they lock you up for a spell into the bargain."

"You mean prison?" I asked, alarmed.

"Absolutely," he said, smacking his lips. "In the clink. Behind the bars. Along with all the other criminals who break the law. *And* a hefty fine into the bargain. Nobody will be more pleased about that than me. I'll see you in court, both of you. You'll be getting a summons to appear."

He turned and walked over to his motorcycle. He flipped the prop stand back into position with his foot and swung his leg over the saddle. Then he kicked the starter and roared off up the road out of sight.

"Phew!" I gasped. "That's done it."

"We was caught," my passenger said. "We was caught good and proper."

"I was caught, you mean."

"That's right," he said. "What you goin' to do now, guv'nor?"

"I'm going straight up to London to talk to my solicitor," I said. I started my car and drove on.

"You mustn't believe what 'ee said to you about goin' to prison," my passenger said. "They don't put somebody in the clink just for speedin'."

"Are you sure of that?" I asked.

"I'm positive," he answered. "They can take your licence away and they can give you a whoppin' big fine, but that'll be the end of it."

I felt tremendously relieved.

"By the way," I said, "why did you lie to him?"

"Who, me?" he said. "What makes you think I lied?"

"You told him you were an unemployed hod carrier. But you told *me* you were in a highly skilled trade."

"So I am," he said. "But it don't do to tell everythin' to a copper."

"So what *do* you do?" I asked him.

"Ah," he said slyly. "That'd be tellin', wouldn't it?"

"Is it something you're ashamed of?"

"Ashamed?" he cried. "Me ashamed of my job? I'm about as proud of it as anybody could be in the entire world!"

"Then why won't you tell me?"

"You writers really is nosy parkers, aren't you?" he said. "And you ain't goin' to be 'appy, I don't think, until you've found out exactly what the answer is?"

"I don't really care one way or the other," I told him, lying.

He gave me a crafty look out of the sides of his eyes. "I think you do care," he said. "I can see it in your face that you think I'm in some kind of very peculiar trade and you're just achin' to know what it is."

I didn't like the way he read my thoughts. I kept quiet and stared at the road ahead.

"You'd be righ' too," he went on. "I *am* in a very peculiar trade. I'm in the queerest peculiar trade of 'em all."

I waited for him to go on.

"That's why I 'as to be extra careful 'oo I'm talking to, you see. 'Ow am I to know, for instance, you're not another copper in plain clothes?"

"Do I look like a copper?"

"No," he said. "You don't. And you ain't. Any fool could tell that."

He took from his pocket a tin of tobacco and a packet of cigarette papers and started to roll a cigarette. I was watching him out of the corner of my eye, and the speed with which he performed this rather difficult operation was incredible. The cigarette was rolled and ready in about five seconds. He ran his tongue along the edge of the paper, stuck it down and popped the cigarette between his lips. Then, as if from nowhere, a lighter appeared in his hand. The lighter flamed. The cigarette was lit. The lighter disappeared. It was altogether a remarkable performance.

"I've never seen anyone roll a cigarette as fast as that," I said.

"Ah," he said, taking a deep suck of smoke. "So you noticed."

"Of course I noticed. It was quite fantastic."

He sat back and smiled. It pleased him very much that I had noticed how quickly he could roll a cigarette. "You want to know what makes me able to do it?" he asked.

"Go on then."

"It's because I've got fantastic fingers. These fingers of mine," he said, holding up both hands high in front of him, "are quicker and cleverer than the fingers of the best piano player in the world!"

"Are you a piano player?"

"Don't be daft," he said. "Do I look like a piano player?"

I glanced at his fingers. They were so beautifully shaped, so slim and long and elegant, they didn't seem to belong to the rest of him at all. They looked the fingers of a brain surgeon or a watchmaker.

"My job," he went on, "is a hundred times more difficult than playin' the piano. Any twerp can learn to do that. There's titchy little kids learnin' to play the piano at almost any 'ouse you go into these days. That's right ain't it?"

"More or less," I said.

"Of course it's right. But there's not one person in ten million can learn to do what I do. Not one in ten million. 'Ow about that?"

"Amazing," I said.

"You're darn right it's amazin'," he said.

"I think I know what you do," I said. "You do conjuring tricks. You're a conjuror."

"Me?" he snorted. "A conjuror? Can you picture me goin' round crummy kids' parties makin' rabbits come out of top 'ats?"

"Then you're a card player. You get people into card games and you deal yourself out marvellous hands."

"Me! A rotten cardsharper!" he cried. "That's a miserable racket if ever there was one."

"All right, I give up."

I was taking the car along slowly now, at no more than forty miles an hour, to make sure I wasn't stopped again. We had come onto the main London-Oxford road and were running down the hill toward Denham.

Suddenly, my passenger was holding up a black leather belt in his hand. "Ever seen this before?" he asked. The belt had a brass buckle of unusual design.

"Hey!" I said. "That's mine, isn't it? It *is* mine! Where did you get it?"

He grinned and waved the belt gently from side to side. "Where d'you think I got it?" He said. "Off the top of your trousers, of course."

I reached down and felt for my belt. It was gone.

"You mean you took it off me while we've been driving along?" I asked, flabbergasted.

He nodded, watching me all the time with those little black ratty eyes.

"That's impossible," I said. "You'd have had to undo the buckle and slide the whole thing out through the loops all the way round. I'd have seen you doing it. And even if I hadn't seen you, I'd have felt it."

"Ah, but you didn't, did you?" he said, triumphant. He dropped the belt on his lap, and now all at once there was a brown shoelace dangling from his fingers. "And what about this, then?" he exclaimed, waving the shoelace.

"What about it?" I said.

"Anyone around 'ere missing a shoelace?" he asked, grinning.

I glanced down at my shoes. The lace of one of them was missing. "Good grief!" I said. "How did you do that? I never saw you bending down."

"You never saw nothin'," he said proudly. "You never even saw me move an inch. And you know why?"

"Yes," I said. "Because you've got fantastic fingers."

"Exactly right!" he cried. "You catch on pretty quick, don't you?" He sat back and sucked away at his homemade cigarette, blowing the smoke out in a thin stream against the windshield. He knew he had impressed me greatly with those two tricks, and this made him very happy. "I don't want to be late," he said. "What time is it?"

"There's a clock in front of you," I told him.

"I don't trust car clocks," he said. "What does your watch say?"

I hitched up my sleeve to look at the watch on my wrist. It wasn't there. I looked at the man. He looked back at me, grinning.

"You've taken that, *too*," I said.

He held out his hand and there was my watch lying in his palm. "Nice bit of stuff, this," he said. "Superior quality. Eighteen-carat gold. Easy to sell, too. It's never any trouble gettin' rid of quality goods."

"I'd like it back, if you don't mind," I said rather huffily.

He placed the watch carefully on the leather tray in front of him. "I wouldn't nick anything from you, guv'nor," he said. "You're my pal. You're giving me a lift."

"I'm glad to hear it," I said.

"All I'm doin' is answerin' your question," he went on. "You asked me what I do for a livin' and I'm showin' you."

"What else have you got of mine?"

He smiled again, and now he started to take from the pocket of his jacket one thing after another that belonged to me – my driver's licence, a key ring with four keys on it, some pound notes, a few coins, a letter from my publishers, my diary, a stubby old pencil, a cigarette lighter, and last of all, a beautiful old sapphire ring with pearls around it belonging to my wife. I was taking the ring up to a jeweller in London because one of the pearls was missing.

"Now *there's* another lovely piece of goods," he said, turning the ring over in his fingers. "That's eighteenth century, if I'm not mistaken, from the reign of King George the Third."

"You're right," I said, impressed. "You're absolutely right."

He put the ring on the leather tray with the other items.

"So you're a pickpocket," I said.

"I don't like that word," he answered. "It's a coarse and vulgar word. Pickpockets is coarse and vulgar people who only do easy little amateur jobs. They lift money from blind old ladies."

"What do you call yourself, then?"

"Me? I'm a fingersmith. I'm a professional fingersmith," He spoke the words solemnly and proudly, as though he were telling me he was President of the Royal College of Surgeons or the Archbishop of Canterbury.

"I've never heard that word before," I said. "Did you invent it?"

"Of course I didn't invent it," he replied. "It's the name given to them who's risen to the very top of the profession. You've heard of a goldsmith or a silversmith, for instance. They're experts with gold and silver. I'm an expert with my fingers, so I'm a fingersmith."

"It must be an interesting job."

"It's a marvellous job," he answered. "It's lovely."

"And that's why you go to the races?"

"Race meetings is easy meat," he said. "You just stand around after the race, watchin' for the lucky ones to queue up and draw their money. And when you see someone collectin' a big bundle of notes, you simply follows 'im and 'elps yourself. But don't get me wrong, guv'nor. I never takes nothin' from a loser. Nor from poor people neither. I only go after them as can afford it, the winners and the rich."

"That's very thoughtful of you," I said. "How often do you get caught?"

"Caught?" he cried, disgusted. "*Me* get caught! It's only pickpockets get caught. Fingersmiths never. Listen, I could take the false teeth out of your mouth if I wanted to and you wouldn't even catch me!"

"I don't have false teeth," I said.

"I know you don't," he answered. "Otherwise I'd 'ave 'em out long ago!"

I believed him. Those long slim fingers of his seemed to be able to do anything.

We drove for a while without talking. "That policeman's going to check up on you pretty thoroughly," I said. "Doesn't that worry you a bit?"

"Nobody's checkin' up on me," he said.

"Of course they are. He's got your name and address written down most carefully in his black book."

The man gave me another of his sly ratty little smiles. "Ah," he said. "So 'ee 'as. But I'll bet 'ee aint got it all written down in 'is memory as well. I've never known a copper yet with a decent memory. Some of 'em can't even remember their own names."

"What's memory got to do with it?" I asked. "It's written down in his book, isn't it?"

"Yes, guv'nor, it is. But the trouble is, 'ee's lost the book. 'Ee's lost both books, the one with my name on it *and* the one with yours."

In the long delicate fingers of his right hand, the man was holding up in triumph the two books he had taken from the policeman's pockets. "Easiest job I ever done," he announced proudly.

I nearly swerved the car into a milk truck, I was so excited.

"That copper's got nothin' on either of us now," he said.

"You're a genius!" I cried.

"'Ee's got no names, no addresses, no car number, no nothin'," he said.

"You're brilliant!"

"I think you'd better pull off this main road as soon as possible," he said. "Then we'd better build a little bonfire and burn these books."

"You're a fantastic fellow!" I exclaimed.

"Thank you, guv'nor, he said. "It's always nice to be appreciated."

SPIDER GEORGE

ALEX SHEARER

S PIDER GEORGE had a bad dream, and so he woke and shouted for his mother.

"Mum, Mum!" he yelled. "Help, come quick!"

"What is it, dear?" she said. "Whatever is the matter?"

"Help," said George. "I'm frightened! There's a person in the room!"

"Oh, George" his mother said. "Not that again. Don't be so silly!"

"No, there is," said George. "There really is!"

His mother looked around the room but could not see anyone.

"Look under the chair!" George said.

She did, but could see nothing.

"It was just a dream, George, that was all."

"It wasn't," said George. "I saw them! It was a nasty person. One of the horrible ones. You know – with two legs!"

"Oh, George," his mother said. "You're imagining it."

"I'm not," George said. "It was coming to get me! Can I come and sleep in your web?"

"Well, try to get back to sleep in your own room first, George. You know when you sleep in our web that you only keep your father awake, snoring and kicking him in the back. Here, I'll tuck you in."

So George's mother tucked him back into his web, which wasn't easy, as he had eight legs. As soon as she got five or six of them tucked in, two or three of them would drop out. But she managed it in the end, and she put on his night-light, and at last he got back to sleep.

At breakfast next morning, George's mum said to his father:

"We're going to have to do something about George. He's frightened of people. In fact, he's got quite a phobia about them."

"Oh, I wouldn't worry too much," George's father said. "He'll grow out of it. When I was his age, I used to be quite frightened of people myself. But they don't bother me now. I still don't like the really big nasty ones, but the little ones are perfectly harmless, and can even be quite useful. They're good at putting the rubbish out, and things like that."

But no sooner had he finished speaking than there was a terrible cry, and a second later, George ran in, in a terrible state of agitation.

"Help, help," he yelled. "I went to use the loo, but there's a person under the toilet seat!"

"Oh, George," his mum said. "You're imagining it."

"I'm not," said George. "There's a person in the toilet bowl. Maybe even two of them. With big teeth. Waiting to bite me on the bottom."

"Come along, George," his mother said. "I'll go with you."

And she went with him and showed him that there were no people there at all.

George played happily by himself for the rest of the morning. His mother took him to the park in the afternoon, where he practised his silk spinning among the trees. After that, he played hide-and-seek and musical webs with his friends, then they went home for tea.

George's mother was in the kitchen taking a packet of frozen flies out of the freezer, when she heard another scream, this time from the bathroom.

She ran there at once.

"What is it, George?" she said. "Whatever is the matter?"

"Look," George said. "Look, look! There's a person in the bath! They must have come up the plughole."

"Honestly, George, there's no one there."

"There is!" George cried. "They've gone now, but there *was* someone. They've gone back down the plughole, that's all. They're waiting to get me at bath time. They live down the plughole and they wait until a poor spider comes by, then they pop up and grab you. And they hit you with a newspaper. Or they pull all your legs off, just for fun."

"Stuff and nonsense," his mother said. "People don't do things like that."

"They do!" George said. "They do! Quick, pour a kettle of hot water down the plughole and make the horrible people go away."

"All right, maybe a few people do nasty things, the ones who don't know any better. But that doesn't mean that *all* people are nasty. I mean, some spiders are nasty too, George. But we're not, are we? We don't go crawling up people's trouser legs and frightening them, do we?"

"No – I suppose not," George agreed.

"Just try not to think about it," his mum said.

"I'll try," George said.

But it wasn't easy. It wasn't easy *not* to think of something at all. For the more you tried not to think of it, the more you did.

When George's dad came home from his web-building business, George's mum told him what had happened that afternoon, and he decided it was time that he and George had a talk.

"Tell me what the problem is, George," he said. "What is it you don't like about people? Why do they frighten you so much, do you think?"

"Well, first, it's their legs," George said. "They've only got two, Dad! They look so strange and creepy they give me the shudders."

"But, George," his dad said, "not everyone has eight legs like us, you know. Why, ladybirds, they only have six legs. And cats, they just have four. And a snail I saw this morning, why, she only had a foot, and the worm that she was talking to had simply no legs at all. And then, on the other side of the coin, there's a millipede out in the garden who has so many legs, he can't even count them all. Because by the time he's counted the ones he's got, he's gone and grown some new ones."

"Yes, I suppose so," George said. "But it's not just that, Dad."

"What else, then?"

"Well, their legs aren't properly hairy. Not like ours. Not like yours and mine and Mum's. Why, Mum's got really nice hairy legs. And it's what they eat too."

"What people eat, you mean?"

"Yes," said George. "They don't eat proper food, do they, not like flies. They have things like chips and fish fingers! Eeeech! I mean, just imagine it, Dad, fish fingers. It's enough to make you ill."

"Yes, I can see what you're getting at, George, and I take your point," his dad said. "But you have to remember that different creatures like to eat different things. And it would never do if we all ate the same food, as there might not be enough to go round. Why, if people lived on flies, the same as we do, they'd scoff the lot and we'd have none. But I agree with you that chips do sound disgusting, and there's nothing I like better myself than a big juicy fly. Flies for breakfast, gnats for tea, and a nice bluebottle sandwich in my lunch box, with a daddy longlegs for afters. But we have to live and let live. And though fish fingers and chips might seem strange to us, to other creatures, nothing could be nicer."

"Yes, Dad, but –" George tried to say, but it was hard to get a word in once his dad had got going.

"Why, a dog I knew once," Dad went on, "when I used to have a web out by the water barrel – I was a single spider in those days, this was before I met your mother – why, that dog, he liked nothing better than a bone. And a sheep of my acquaintance, she was very fond of grass. Now grass isn't my cup of tea, in fact, I don't like cups of tea at all. I much prefer a dew drop, or a spot of rain on a leaf. And –"

"Yes, I know, Dad," George said. "But it's not just that, it's the way people stand on the *floor*, instead of living halfway up the wall, or dangling from the ceiling, like they ought to. They just don't know how to behave or have any manners at all."

"Hmm, maybe so," Dad said. "But what you have to remember is that, often, people are just as afraid of spiders as spiders are of people."

"Yes, Dad," George said. "If you say so." But he didn't really believe it.

Because how could a person be afraid of a spider? People were huge, and spiders were tiny, even the biggest of them was nowhere near the size of a person. People couldn't be afraid of spiders, could they? Especially the ones as small as George, who wasn't even big enough yet to catch flies.

It was ridiculous. He couldn't believe that.

But that night, George woke again with the horrors, and his mum had to go and comfort him.

"There's a person in the wardrobe!" he said. "And it's coming to get me!"

"Oh, George," his mum said, opening the wardrobe door, so that he could see there was nothing there. "What are we going to do with you!"

And it was ages before he could get back to sleep. His mum had to stay with him, singing him spider lullabyes called Spiderbyes, and telling him his favourite stories, such as "Spider In Boots", "Rumple-spider-skin", "The Spider and the Pea" and "The Spider's New Clothes". And it was only after she had told him the story of "The Spider and the Seven Dwarfs" and had sung him "Rudolph the Red Nosed Spider" – both of which were his favourites – that he finally went to sleep.

Now things could have gone on forever like this, and Spider George might have remained frightened of people for the rest of his life, had he not run into another George – George the boy.

Spider George had gone off exploring in the garden, and he had found himself by a wall. Now in the wall was a drainpipe. And as George was a curious spider, and as no one had told him not to, he decided to crawl up the drainpipe to investigate, and to see what he might discover.

At first, everything was in darkness, and George became afraid that he might meet something nasty, coming the other way. But then he saw some light, at the far end of the tunnel, and he headed for it, to see what might be there. On he went, climbing upwards, finally to emerge from the top of the pipe into what seemed like a great big empty swimming pool, which had been drained of water.

George looked up then, and just above his head he saw two of the most enormous taps he had ever seen in his life. But he recognized them at once, and he scurried up to have a good look at them, and just as he expected, one of the taps was marked with the letter H for Hot, and the other was marked with the letter C for Cold. And standing next to the taps, in a huge dish, was the largest cake of soap he had ever come across.

"It's a bath!" George thought. "I'm in the bath. I've come up the plughole. But what sort of creature could have a bath like this? It must be the biggest spider in the world to have a bath this size. It must be the greatest spider ever seen." He went for a walk around. "Yes, it must be King of all the Spiders! The Emperor, even! Or maybe it's a giant spider, as in 'Incy and the Beanstalk', or maybe –"

But then a chilling, terrifying thought came into his head – "maybe this bath belongs to –

– a PERSON!"

As soon as the thought came into his mind, George leaped down from the side of the bath and made a run for the plughole, so as to get back down the drainpipe, as quickly as he could.

He must have been halfway there when he heard a noise. He glanced up to see the bathroom door opening, but he didn't stop running.

Then he heard a voice, a great booming voice that stopped him in his tracks.

"George –" the voice said, and for a moment George thought that the voice was talking to him. But then he realized that it wasn't talking to him at all. It was talking to a boy who had just come into the bathroom. A boy with the same name as himself.

"George!" the great voice boomed – at least it sounded like a great voice to a spider, though to a person it probably sounded quite ordinary. "Go and get ready for your bath, please. I'll be in to run it in a minute."

And of course Spider George knew then that the voice belonged to the boy's mother.

He ran as fast as he could to get to the plughole before he was seen. But he wasn't quick enough. A shadow fell over the bath, and George stopped in his tracks, frozen with fear.

This was it.

His worst nightmare.

All his bad dreams come true.

It was –

– a person!

Coming to get him.

George looked up. He saw two big eyes looking down at him. Not nice kind spider's eyes, either, but big, bulgy person's eyes. They may have only been a child's eyes, but they looked big to a spider, just the same.

For a second George was too afraid to move, too afraid to scream. This was it. It was going to happen. The boy was going to pick him up and pull his legs off. This was the end. George braced himself for it.

"If only my Mum and Dad were here to save me," he thought. But he was on his own.

And then a most curious thing happened. Instead of picking him up and pulling his legs off, the boy just stood there for a moment, frozen, just as George was frozen, and seemingly unable to move.

Then slowly the boy moved his hand, and he pointed at George with his finger, and he uttered the one word.

"Spider!" he said.

And he yelled so loudly that the soap dish fell off the side of the bath.

George was puzzled.

"Spider?" he thought. "Where's the spider? That boy seems

to be afraid of a spider somewhere. I wonder where it is? It must be a pretty big spider, to frighten a boy like that."

And George looked around to see where the big spider was, the one that frightened the boy so much, but there was none to be seen.

The boy was yelling very loudly now. And not only was he yelling, he was jumping up and down, and even starting to cry.

"Spider! Spider!" he yelled. "Mum, Mum! Come quick! There's a spider in the bath!"

Spider George heard footsteps hurrying, and a voice saying, "Oh, George, not again!" And when he looked up, it was now to see two pairs of bulgy eyeballs looking down at him. There was the big pair and an even bigger pair as well, which seemed to be hidden behind two windows.

"Good heavens," thought George. "That must be the boy's mother. And look, she's got her own windows! I've never seen a person with their own windows to look out of before. How amazing. Why, if that boy's mother has got windows, then she must be a house. Fancy having a house for your mum. How amazing."

"Spider! Spider!" the boy kept shouting. "There's a spider in the bath!"

When George heard the boy going on shouting like this, he began to feel rather important.

"If I'm so small, and a big chap like that is afraid of me," he thought. "I must be more special than I look."

And out of sheer devilment, he puffed himself up to his full size, and he tried to growl and to look fierce, and he showed all his teeth at once, in the hope that he might make the boy even more frightened, and then frighten his mother as well.

"Spider! Spider!" the boy said. "Nasty spider in the bath!"

But George wasn't able to frighten the boy's mother too.

"Oh, honestly," she said. "That's nothing to be afraid of. A tiny little thing like that!"

"It'll run up my trousers," the boy said. "And bite me on the bottom."

"Oh, really, don't be so silly. It's a harmless little spider, that's all."

"Harmless?" thought George. "Not me. I'm rough and tough and dangerous through and through."

"Kill it!" the boy said. "Squash it with a newspaper! Pull its legs off!"

"Certainly not," his mother said. "I'll put it out of the window."

Two huge hands descended then. George ran for the plughole. But he wasn't fast enough and the hands were upon him before he could get there.

"It really is the end," George thought. "It really is. Goodbye cruel world. It was a short life, but a sweet one. It's a pity I never got a chance to grow up, that's all. Goodbye Mum. Goodbye Dad. Goodbye all the flies I never ate. I knew it would happen. My worst dream has come true. A person is going to get me!"

But to his amazement, the hands neither squashed him, nor crushed him, nor pulled off his legs. Instead, they very gently scooped him up, and tenderly carried him to the window.

And oddly, George didn't feel afraid.

"This person," he thought, "isn't afraid of me. And I am not afraid of them. For spiders and people can be friends."

The boy's mother opened the bathroom window, and she dropped George out into the air.

The breeze took him, and he descended on a line of spun silk, and he glided right back down to where he had started. And when he landed, he saw his own mother waiting there for him.

"George," she said, "I've been looking for you. I wondered where you had gone."

George told his mother nothing about his adventures. He kept them to himself as his own personal secret. For children come to an age when they don't want to tell their parents everything, and they wish to have private things for themselves.

His mother did notice something different about him though, and she remarked on it to George's father some days later.

"You know," she said, "George seems to have stopped having bad dreams. He hasn't woken up in the night for ages. He doesn't seem to have nightmares any more or worry about people coming to get him. I wonder why that is."

"It's probably the little chat I had with him," George's father said. "It must have put his mind at rest."

And he felt rather pleased with himself, that he had solved the problem of George's nightmares.

As for George, he slept as soundly as a log. He was no longer afraid of people, and he hoped that they would no longer be afraid of him. But as he got older, sometimes, out of pure mischief, George would creep up on a little girl or a little boy, and he would go, "Boo!" And he would roll his eyes and waggle all his legs at once, and show all of his teeth. And nine times out of ten, the little boy or the little girl would scream and run away, shouting:

"Ahhh! Ahhh! It's a spider!"

And when they did this, George would laugh, and laugh, and laugh, until the tears ran down his face, and down over his eight hairy legs.

For, to this day, he still can't understand why something as big as a person should be afraid of something as small as a spider.

But it does make him laugh.

And it does make him wonder.

And one thing is for certain – he isn't frightened of people any more.

And he never will be again.

ACKNOWLEDGEMENTS

The publisher would like to thank the copyright holders for permission to reproduce the following copyright material:

Allan Ahlberg: Extract from *Woof!* by Allan Ahlberg (Viking, 1986). Text copyright © Allan Ahlberg 1986. Reproduced by permission of Penguin Books Ltd. **Judy Blume**: Extract from *Double Fudge* by Judy Blume (Macmillan, 2002). Copyright © 2002 by Judy Blume. Reprinted by permission of William Morris Agency, Inc. on behalf of the Author. **Richmal Crompton**: "William's New Year's Day" from *Just William* by Richmal Crompton. Copyright © Richmal C. Ashbee. Reprinted by permission of Macmillan Children's Books, London, UK. **Roald Dahl**: "The Hitchhiker" from *The Wonderful Story of Henry Sugar* by Roald Dahl (Jonathan Cape and Penguin Books Ltd). Copyright © Roald Dahl, 1977. Reprinted by permission of David Higham Associates Ltd. **Morris Gleitzman**: Extract from *Blabber Mouth* by Morris Gleitzman (Macmillan, 1992). Copyright © 1992 Gleitzman McCaul Pty Ltd. Reprinted by permission of Macmillan Children's Books, London, UK. **M. L. Greenall**: "Harry the Street Pigeon" by M. L. Greenall from *Story of the Year Book 5* (Scholastic, 1997). Copyright © M. L. Greenall 1997. Reprinted by permission of the author. **Andy Griffiths**: "In the Shower with Andy" from *Just Annoying* by Andy Griffiths (Macmillan, 1998). Copyright © Andy Griffiths 1998. Reprinted by permission of Macmillan Children's Books, London, UK and by arrangement with the copyright holder, Andy Griffiths c/o Curtis Brown (Aust) Pty Ltd. **Russell Hoban**: *How Tom Beat Captain Najork and his Hired Sportsmen* by Russell Hoban (Red Fox). Copyright © Russell Hoban 1974. Reprinted by permission of David Higham Associates Ltd. **Paul Jennings**: "Wunderpants" from *Unreal!* by Paul Jennings (Penguin Books Australia, 1985). Copyright © Paul Jennings 1985. Reprinted by permission of Penguin Books Australia Ltd. **Terry Jones**: "The Ship of Fools" from *Fantastic Stories* by Terry Jones (Chrysalis, 1992). Copyright © Terry Jones 1992. Reprinted by permission of Chrysalis Children's Books. **Dick King-Smith**: Extract from *Julius Caesar's Goat* by Dick King-Smith (Puffin, 2000). Copyright © Fox Busters Ltd 2000. Reprinted by permission of A.P. Watt Ltd on behalf of Fox Busters Ltd. **Errol Lloyd**: "The Ratcatcher" by Errol Lloyd from *The Much Better*

FUNNY STORIES

Chosen by Michael Rosen

Laugh until you drop!

Michael Rosen brings together thirty-nine of the world's
funniest stories in one side-splitting volume. There's classic
comedy from the likes of James Thurber, Joyce Grenfell,
Roald Dahl, Roger McGough and Ann Cameron, as well as
a good helping of giggle-inducing folktales from as far apart
as Norway and Pakistan.

". . . something to make almost everyone laugh."
– CHILDREN'S BOOKS OF THE YEAR

"A very rich collection."
– BOOKS FOR YOUR CHILDREN

ISBN: 0 86272 801 0

Titles in the Story Library Series